MW01064012

*"Who's Who In Interior Design" Presents*

# 100 DESIGNERS' FAVORITE ROOMS

SECOND EDITION

John L. Pellam

Foreword by Vicente Wolf

Barons Who's Who

SELECTED PROJECTS OF THE WORLD'S FINEST DESIGNERS & ARCHITECTS

*NORTH AMERICA • EUROPE • ASIA • SOUTH AMERICA • THE MIDDLE EAST*

*Page one:* Vicki Wenger (design), Gordon Beall (photog.); *page two:* Geoffrey Bradfield (design), H. Durston Saylor (photog.); *title page:* Samuel Botero (design), Phillip Ennis (photog.); *page four:* Geoffrey Bradfield (design), H. Durston Saylor (photog.); *contents page:* Samuel Botero (design), Phillip Ennis (photog.); *page 224:* Michael de Santis (design), Phillip Ennis (photog.).

Distributed worldwide by Baker + Taylor International
652 East Main Street, Bridgewater, New Jersey 08807
(908) 218-0400. Fax: (908) 707-4387

Published by Barons Who's Who
412 North Coast Highway, B-110, Laguna Beach, California 92651
(714) 497-8615. Fax: (714) 786-8918

10 9 8 7 6 5 4 3 2 1

Library of Congress Catalogue Number 94-071871
International Standard Book Number 1-882292-03-0

Typography by Prep Graphics, Laguna Hills, California
Printed and bound in Hong Kong

# *CONTENTS*

# FOREWORD

This book showcases one hundred designers and their favorite rooms. The many rooms are as diversified and as intriguing as the designers themselves. There are many different styles represented, from traditional to modern to transitional in-between. Some are serious, some whimsical, others are utterly classy while still others have a quality of rustic country charm. Each designer has chosen their favorite room, one that is memorable and makes a certain statement: a statement of style as well as a statement about the designer.

One of the purposes of this book is to give each reader a selection of some of the top designers from around the world, including North and South America, Asia, Europe and the Middle East. It is fascinating to see the influences of different cultures on interior design and to be able to compare the talents of those international designers, all within the same medium. All of these designers work on an international scale and are capable of working within the United States as well as abroad. Therefore, there should be no hesitation on your part when considering a designer from outside your area.

In selecting a designer, one should approach the task as if one were seeking out a portrait artist. Select the style that most appeals to you, and then have the artist create an interpretation of how they perceive you. Working with a designer is an intensely personal experience. The designer brings to the project an innate sensibility which comes from a true and meaningful understanding of the client's needs and desires. This enables him/her to create a job that has been tailored to the environment of the individual.

When selecting my "favorite" room, I chose a room that most represented my point of view: a space that would be timeless and would always have a fresh and clean look. Other designers use their own criteria for selecting their favorite room. The selections and comments in this book give a sense of who the designers are and what they believe in. This unique format gives you background information on the designer, and in his/her own words, remarks regarding the project they chose and why it was chosen as their favorite.

When looking at the following pages, be aware of the limitations and constraints the designer has in completing the selected project. In the majority of cases, the designer does not have a totally free hand. Rather, he/she must design projects that fit the needs and criteria of their clients, whether it be a residential project, a hotel, restaurant, office or contract design. Consequently, a compromise between creativity and necessity must be reached. A talented designer is one who can work within these boundaries, yet create a project that is original and resourceful.

Among the myriad choices given in this book, it should be easy for the reader to select a designer whose style is compatible with their own. Sit back and enjoy your journey into the fabulous world of architectural and interior design. When you're done, I'm sure you'll find your favorite.

*Vicente Wolf*

*A sleek polished steel and black granite console contrasts with traditional coromandel screen, antique Chinese philosopher and lacquered side chairs. Interior design: Rodger Dobbel, ASID. Photography: Mark Darley.*

# *INTRODUCTION*

This Second Edition of *100 Designers' Favorite Rooms* is presented to you as an international portfolio of the finest work of the world's leading interior and architectural designers. One hundred designers are featured, each displaying their favorite design project. Inherent in the very nature of this book is diversity in both style and geography. Thus, the following pages have been divided into four sections: North America East, North America West, International, and Worldwide Contract Design. The first three sections feature residential projects in their respective geographical areas, while the fourth presents commercial design projects from throughout the world. So that you may easily use this book to select your next interior or architectural designer, this volume includes a complete contact directory of all featured designers.

• • • • •

I'd like you to think of the following two hundred-plus pages as a world tour, taking you to exotic cities around the globe, and into the world's most beautifully designed homes, galleries, offices and hotels. You begin your tour with residential designs, where you'll see the interiors of homes, penthouses and estates throughout the major cities of North America – New York, Toronto, Miami, Washington, Beverly Hills, San Francisco, Mexico City, Dallas, Memphis, Chicago, Atlanta, San Diego and many others. In the International section you'll journey from a desert palace in the United Arab Emirates to a fabulous riverfront penthouse in Bangkok, from an incredible seaside estate in Barbados, to a *toreador's* home – complete with bullring – outside Mexico City, and then on to beautiful private homes in Hong Kong, Istanbul, Taipei, Caracas, Rio de Janeiro, Jakarta, Jeddah and the English countryside. Next you're off to see the world's finest hotels, offices, and commercial centers. You'll tour the Grand Salon of Honor in Tunis, the exquisite Bistro Restaurant in the Mirage Hotel in Las Vegas; you'll see the Ritz-Carlton in Cancun, and the stunning ultra-modern air terminal in Hinada, Japan, as well as the wonderful renovation of Philadelphia's Bellvue Hotel, the beautiful design of the Sandals La Toc Hotel in St. Lucia, West Indies, China's exotic Beijing Gloria Plaza Hotel and the restoration of Thailand's remarkable Chalermkrung Royal Theatre, along with a tour of other commercial designs in Europe, North and South America, Asia and the Middle East.

As you travel the globe, you'll be introduced to one hundred of the world's most creative and talented designers and architects – world class professionals on the cutting edge of the newest ideas in international design. As you meet each designer, you'll see their finest work, listen as they explain why the room shown is their favorite, and learn what design innovations they employed to overcome the challenges each room presented. When your tour is completed, you'll have discovered an abundance of new design ideas. And if your journey has been successful, by the time you return to your own home you'll have at least one designer or architect in mind for your next interior design project – a project that could easily become that designer's new favorite!

*John L. Pellam*

*From the Kips Bay Boys' and Girls' Club Decorator Showhouse: a dramatic effect is achieved using suspended theater spotlights to showcase this spacious interior. Interior design: Michael de Santis, ASID. Photography: Jamie Ardiles-Arce.*

# THE MAJOR DESIGN ASSOCIATIONS

Because many of the designers featured within this volume are members of one or more professional design associations, a brief explanation of the purposes and goals of a representative number of these organizations is offered upon the following pages. The American Institute of Architects (AIA), the American Society of Interior Designers (ASID), the Institute of Business Designers (IBD), and the International Society of Interior Designers (ISID) have each submitted the information on their respective organizations presented here.

Other pertinent organizations of which featured designers are members include the Architectural Institute of Japan (AIJ), the Barbados Institute of Architects (BIA), the Chartered Society of Designers (CSD), the Chinese Society of Interior Designers (CSID), the German Interior Architects Association (BDIA), the Himpunan Design Interior Indonesia (HDII), the Hong Kong Institute of Architects (HKIA), the Indonesian Architectural Association (Ikatan Arsitek Indonesia) (IAI), the Interior Decorators & Designers Association (IDDA), the Interior Design Guild (IDG), the International Design & Furnishings Association (IDFA), the Jamaican Institute of Architects (JIA), the Japan Institute of Architects (JIA), the Japan Institute of Design (JID), the Korean Society of Interior Designers (KSID), the l'Ordre des Architects Libanais (OAL), the l'Ordre des Architects Syriens (OAS), the Malaysian Institute of Interior Design (MIID), the Mexican Chamber of Architectural Construction (MCAC), the National Trust for Historic Preservation, the Royal Australian Institute of Architects (RAIA), the Royal Institute of British Architects (RIBA), and the Singapore Institute of Architects (SIA). Professional status within an organization is indicated when the initials of the design organization follow a designer's name. Members achieving Professional status have fulfilled exacting education and experience requirements and, for a number of organizations, have passed a nationally administered examination testing a comprehensive range of design principles and standards. Fellow membership (e.g.: FASID) is an esteemed recognition granted to those designers who have exhibited outstanding professional conduct, expertise and participation within their organizations.

These design organizations have set the highest standards of quality, service and competence for their members, and provide and encourage continued education in all aspects of architectural and interior design. To this end, specific entities have been created to regulate and monitor the interior design profession. The National Council for Interior Design Qualification (NCIDQ) administers qualifying examinations, the passage of which are required by many organizations in order to receive a 'Professional' designation. The Foundation for Interior Design Education Research (FIDER) is governed by design practitioners and educators from the American Society of Interior Designers, the Interior Design Educators Council, the Institute of Business Designers and the Interior Designers of Canada. This foundation handles special accreditation of interior design education offered at institutions of higher education throughout the United States and Canada.

*Mirrored panels, walls and ceiling create a sparkling and multi-dimensional illusion of expanse in the narrow hallway of this New York penthouse. Interior design: Carol Meltzer, ASID. Photography: James Levin.*

# *The American Institute of Architects*

Headquartered in Washington, D.C., The American Institute of Architects (AIA) is the preeminent professional association representing America's architects since 1957. More than 55,000 members adhere to a Code of Ethics and Professional Conduct that assures the client, the public, and colleagues of an architect's dedication to the highest standards in professional practice.

Through public outreach, education, and government affairs initiatives, the AIA works to serve its membership and the public at large. Community design and development initiatives encourage well-designed, affordable housing for all Americans. By forging coalitions of architects, community leaders, and representatives of other professional disciplines, the AIA works to create urban environments that are inviting, affirming expressions of community life. By speaking with a united voice, architects in the AIA can also influence government decisions that affect the practice of the profession and quality of American life. Together with its more than 300 state and local organizations, the Institute promotes public and professional betterment through legislative advocacies such as accessibility to all Americans and protection of the nation's neglected infrastructure.

The Institute serves its members with professional development opportunities, information services, personal benefits, and client-oriented resources. Contract documents developed and revised by the AIA are the model for the design and construction industry. And programs such as the Intern-Architect Development Program, registration-exam preparation courses, and employment referral services serve architecture students and future architects. AIA members also participate in volunteer professional committees specializing in such arenas as design, interiors, education, the environment, housing, regional and urban design, and historic resources. Among the broad range of AIA professional interest areas, the Interiors program establishes vital links with various services and approaches within the interiors community, and develops liaisons with manufacturers and custom-service providers on quality, cost, and environmental issues. The Institute also hosts a "Design Excellence in the Architecture of Interiors" initiative, to help interior architects recognize and embrace the linkage between competency, success, innovation, and excellence in view of increasing competition in a global marketplace.

Nationally recognized AIA awards programs set the standard for architectural excellence while cultivating an ever-growing audience for good design. The annual event, "Accent on Architecture," publicly celebrates design excellence, while the AIA Fellowship Program recognizes notable contributions of its members. In partnership with The American Architectural Foundation (AAF), the AIA strives for a national design literacy in the belief that a well-trained, creative profession and an informed public are prerequisites for an enhanced quality of American life.

*The natural wood conference table and green carpeting create a crisp and professional image for the Winbond Electronics Corporation boardroom in Taipei. Interior design by AIA member Joshua Pan, photography by Y.C. Chien.*

# *The American Society of Interior Designers*

The need to establish high qualifications for design practitioners is driven by the need for comprehensive knowledge about the proximate environment and emerging new design technologies.

Designers of skill, creative insight, and thorough technical expertise are required to protect the investments and safety of consumers – both in the contract and residential arenas. To that end, ASID offers an educational career path to its members which is open to students, beginning practitioners and to experienced professionals.

The Society's continuing education program is un-rivaled in terms of depth and scope – designers may avail themselves of some forty professional development seminars conducted throughout the nation.

These courses provide the technical and business skills necessary to keep abreast of the changes which are shaping the future of the profession and of the American interior.

More than ever before, as the field of interior design expands and becomes increasingly more complex, design professionals and their clients need an organization which can do two crucial things: first, properly and fairly represent them; secondly, provide a voice for legislation that will protect the public and enhance the practice of interior design. ASID – through its programs in communications, education, legislative and public affairs, membership and industry – provides that cohesive support and representation.

Today, the highest mark of the professional standard is conferred by the letters – ASID (American Society of Interior Designers). Through accredited education, documented experience, and adherence to a code of ethics, it is the ASID interior designer who commands the confidence of consumers and the respect of the professional design community. Professional members – the highest category of membership – are identified by the letters ASID after their names. Professional members must complete a national examination in addition to meeting criteria regarding education and experience required for Allied and Associate members.

*Inspired by the client's collection of contemporary sculpture, a unique yet traditional design approach was created for this one room studio in New York City. Interior design by ASID member Michael Love, photography by Peter Blake.*

# *The Institute of Business Designers*

Founded in 1969, the Institute of Business Designers (IBD) was established because of the growing demand for an organization devoted exclusively to the profession of commercial design. The objective of the Institute is to unite and advance the profession of commercial interior design through advocacy of ethical standards and through legislative and regulatory activities, the expansion of the influence of our members; through education, the leadership and professional development of our members, and the protection of the health, safety and welfare of the public; through networking, a common meeting ground for the exchange of ideas and the development of professional relationships; through public relations, the enhancement of the public's understanding of the value and scope of our members' expertise.

The organization represents a network of over 5,300 members, linked nationally and locally in thirty-seven chapters across the United States. Individuals are either Professional, Affiliate, Allied or Student members, as appropriate to level of training and experience. Professional members must be actively engaged in commercial interior design and have been certified by NCIDQ or by The Governing Board for Contract Interior Design Standards. Affiliate members are actively engaged in commercial interior design and have completed either a minimum of two years of design training at a recognized design school or college or a minimum of four years design experience which includes dealing directly with the public. Allied members are those interested in the field of commercial interior design, but who are not engaged in the provision of design services and/or have never qualified for Professional membership in the Institute. Student members must be currently enrolled in an accredited two, three, four, or five year interior design program. IBD also encourages Corporate membership for those organizations interested in commercial interior design, but whose main functions are not the provision of design services. This may include, but is not limited to, manufacturing firms, design centers, and schools. IBD membership benefits include accredited educational courses offering Continuing Education Units, leadership experience through chapter and national committees, insurance services, and legislative support at the national level through the National Legislative Coalition for Interior Design. Additionally, members receive Perspective, IBD's national quarterly publication. The magazine contains articles and information about local and national activities related to the field of interior design. IBD also publishes a technical publication called Industry-In-Depth, which is designed as an educational tool for interior specification and the professional practice of commercial interior design. Industry-In-Depth is published periodically throughout the year. IBD also sponsors two of the nation's premier commercial design competitions – the IBD/Interior Design magazine Contract Design Competition and the IBD/Contract Design magazine Product Design Competition. IBD also sponsors the Will Ching, FIBD Design Award, established to recognize excellence in design by firms with five or fewer designers.

---

*Adapted reuse transformed this warehouse into a two-level commercial space, with a suite of business offices situated above a lower level design and art studio. Interior design by IBD member Cynthia Leftwich, photography by Robert Suddarth.*

# The International Society of Interior Designers

The International Society of Interior Designers (ISID) was founded by a group of nine Los Angeles based professional interior designers and chartered in January 1979 in the State of California. A worldwide membership supports the following purposes:

- Legal recognition of professional interior designers in order to protect the health and welfare of the consumer and to protect against fraud and malpractice;
- Implementation of laws and studies in design to benefit aged, infirm and physically impaired;
- Ongoing education for the interior designer through seminars, lectures and academic courses;
- Development of educational programs for students in accredited schools of interior design, participation in apprenticeship and placement counseling;
- Scholarships and awards;
- Participation in an exchange of international design ideas, products and trends;
- Involvement in civic, community, national and international projects through technical advice and assistance to the deprived;
- Participation in restoration and preservation of historical, cultural and architectural sites;
- Development of liaisons, coordination of mutual goals and improvement in lines of communication with schools of environmental design;
- And promotion of networking, on an international level, between designers, students, trade and related fields.

*The ISID also sponsors:*

- Lectures, seminars and conferences to stimulate and enrich members' careers.
- A networking system which provides members the opportunity to enjoy personal ties and long lasting relationships.
- International exchange to encourage communication amongst members in cities and countries throughout the world for professional assistance fellowship.
- Chapter activities, including civic, community and charitable projects, monthly meetings, social events and year round educational programs.
- Publication of newsletters, keeping members current as to news, calendars and other events.
- Design houses, which enable members to showcase their talents and products.
- Awards in Fellowship, Student Scholarship, Chapter, Personal Development, and Trade categories.

*Empire green walls, amethyst silk damask and marbleized frieze complement the regency mahogany and gilt furnishings in this elegant Chicago dining room. Interior design by ISID member Rod Maxwell, photography by Steve Donisch.*

# *NORTH AMERICA: EAST*

***Anita-Louise Aiello, ARIDO, ASID,*** Formal Dining Room, Ontario

***Dale Anderson, ASID,*** Elm Paneled Library, Chicago Area

***Tapati Dali Basu, ASID,*** Traditional Living Room, West Hartford

***Samuel Botero,*** Sutton Place Living Room, New York City

***Geoffrey N. Bradfield, ASID,*** Penthouse Entry/Living Room, Calgary

***Alfredo Brito,*** Contemporary Living Room, Miami

***Ruth-Virginia Burt,*** Fifth Avenue Master Bedroom, New York

***Barbara Jean Campbell, ASID,*** Mediterranean Wine Room, Potomac

***Michael de Santis, ASID,*** Contemporary Living Room, Palm Beach Gardens

***Robert Dirstein,*** Traditional Living Room, Toronto

***Trudy Dujardin, ASID,*** Living Room/Mezzanine, Nantucket Island Shore

***Susanne E. Eisinger, ASID,*** Traditional Living Room, Alexandria

***William R. Eubanks,*** Traditional Drawing Room, Memphis

***Elwyn Colby Ferris,*** Romantic Bedroom, Washington DC

***Landy Gardner,*** Conservatory, Nashville

***Chip Johnston, ASID, IFDA,*** Traditional Living Room, Atlanta

***Judith Sisler Johnston,*** Contemporary Living Room, Florida

***Debra S. Kelley,*** Contemporary Living Room, Hilton Head Island

***Patricia A. Lazor, Allied ASID,*** Traditional Library, New Jersey

***Michael Love, ASID,*** Contemporary Living Room, New York City

***Emma Matienzo-Smeal, Allied ASID,*** Traditional Living Room, Longwood

***Rod Maxwell, ISID,*** Victorian Guest Room, Chicago

***H. Glenn McGee, AIA, ASID,*** Traditional Living/Dining Room, Chattanooga

***Carol Meltzer, ASID,*** Penthouse Living Room, New York City

***Noranit Tui Pranich, ASID,*** Contemporary Living Room, Palm Beach

***Sandi Samole, ASID, IDG,*** Modern Living/Dining Room, Miami

***Darryl H. Savage,*** Transitional Bedroom, Annapolis

***Patricia S. Stotler,*** Contemporary Living/Dining Room, Palm Beach

***Vicki Wenger, ASID,*** Traditional Entry, Washington DC

***Vicente Wolf,*** Living Room, Richland Plantation, Natchez

*The rich combination of mahogany chairs, tapestry, formal painting, and glass top wrought iron table transforms this breakfast area into a dramatic and elegant room. Interior design: Alfredo Brito. Photography: Dan Forer.*

# Anita-Louise Aiello, ARIDO

Managing a healthy combination of both commercial and residential design, Anita-Louise Aiello is founder and principal owner of one of Canada's leading firms, Design Concepts. Since its inception in 1983, under the strong leadership of Ms. Aiello, a wide variety of interiors ranging from corporate facilities across the country, retail and institutional projects of varying complexity, and countless residential interiors of every style have been successfully completed. Her work as a Resident Guest Expert on Toronto's CityLine live television program can be seen monthly, where she shares concepts of good design with a live studio audience. Ms. Aiello participates in community projects such as numerous Ronald McDonald Houses, and gives her time to professional development, holding various board positions for NCIDQ over the past seven years and, more recently, Canada's liaison with NLCID. She prides herself in her ability to achieve an interior which reflects the individuality and style of her clients, while providing exemplary quality and service.

"An appealing blend of furniture and art gives this room its warmth and charm. With a spectacular view of the seven hundred acre estate from the dining room within this fifteen thousand square foot residence, my challenge was to indulge the client with an interior that compliments this estate. Architectural focus has been designed into the intricate plaster ceiling and frieze, delicately faux finished to accentuate its detail. Distinguished elements, such as elegant period style furnishings, along with antique light fixtures and oil paintings, enhance this pleasurable dining experience. Each piece carefully complements the other, combining a personal philosophy of blended architectural elements of good design."

*Anita-Louise Aiello, ARIDO, ASID, Design Concepts*
*5045 Orbitor Drive, Suite 400, Building 12, Mississuaga, Ontario L4W 4Y4*
*Tel.: (905) 602-7075, Fax: (905) 602-7073*

*Photography: Keith Franklin*

# Dale Carol Anderson, ASID

Dale Carol Anderson is an award-winning designer who has been published in *How to Work with an Interior Designer, Showcase of Interior Design (Midwest Edition), Town & Country, Better Homes & Gardens'* special interest magazines and the *Chicago Tribune*.

"Interior design, at its best, is a synthesis of the architecture and the site, the craftsmen and artisans and the needs of the client, interpreted by a professional, trained to pull it all together," Ms. Anderson states. "To me, attention to detail is what distinguishes a quality design project – dressmaker touches, for example, like the relationship of the size of a sofa arm to its skirt, welting, whether to use brush fringe or none. But detail doesn't only mean adding, it's also knowing when to edit. What makes a room timeless is staying away from trends, choosing classic pieces with strong proportions that will look good in twenty years."

"I love the warmth of this room. It's more elegant than casual, but it's so relaxing, a put-up-your-feet space. And, it's intimate in spite of the twelve-foot ceilings and large scale of the furnishings. The details of Louis XIV-style elm paneling are a soft backdrop for a striking mix of primitive pieces from all over the world: an ancient Syrian mosaic that serves as a table on a custom-designed iron base, pre-Colombian sculpture, Bolivian silver, African textiles, African bronze sculptures and a powerful carved armoire from the jungles of South America. What you don't see are the built-in conveniences. Hidden within the decor is a wet bar, a motorized TV screen and another forty-two inch TV. Comfortable seating is provided by the two oversized leather sofas. Decorative ottomans and throw pillows add to the charm of the setting, with its fireplace, wood beam ceiling and wood floors. This design marries creature comforts with style in a beautiful livable space."

*Dale Anderson, ASID, Dale Carol Anderson Ltd.*
*2030 North Magnolia Avenue, Chicago, Illinois 60614*
*Tel.: (312) 348-5200, Fax: (312) 348-5271*

*Photography: Tony Soluri*

*Photography: Tom Cliff*

# Tapati Dali Basu, ASID

Dali Basu originally studied architecture and worked for the School of Planning and Architecture in Delhi, India. She came to the United States after marriage and graduated with a degree in Interior Design from the University of Hartford in 1973. Since that time, Mrs. Basu has been working in interior design and remodeling, including both commercial and residential projects. She has given numerous lectures on "Color and its Versatility" and other topics relating to color at various conferences in New England. She is a licensed interior designer by the State of Connecticut and a member of the West Hartford Chamber of Commerce as well as the National Trust for Historic Preservation in Washington DC.

"Color has always fascinated me; since childhood, color and creating designs have been a part of my dream. After completing my study in interior design, the creative and effective utilization of color has become an integral part of my design style. This project is a union of Oriental and western elements brought together into a unique blend. In this living room, I have attempted to capture both the vitality and optimism that is so much a part of the American spirit, and combined it with the subtlety of Oriental style. The room combines both Indian and western aspects. The structure reflects the Renaissance period with its french doors and windows, cathedral ceilings, curved staircase and marble fireplace. The decorating adds the flair of India and the Orient with its vivid color. I believe that the process of creativity is a never ending journey of discovery."

*Tapati Dali Basu, ASID*
*46 Ferncliff Drive, West Hartford, Connecticut 06117*
*Tel.: (203) 232-9713*

# Samuel Botero

For over twenty years, as one of New York's leading interior designers, Samuel Botero has been responsible for creating both inventive and innovative interiors for his international clientele. From a very early point in his career, Mr. Botero has been involved in luxury residential projects, such as the various residences for Princess Yasmin Aga Khan, Mr. and Mrs. Michael Schulhof, and Mr. and Mrs. Raul Julia. Mr. Botero prides himself on inspiring his diversified customers into expanding their own individual, creative and aesthetic sensitivities. His dedication to the art of living combined with his eclectic taste, has evolved into the "Botero Collection", which encompasses fine furniture, lighting, accessories, art and antiques.

"I love my Sutton Place living room in New York City because it exemplifies my personal philosophy of design. It is a fantasy room. It is a very intimate and personal space, which allows me to be inspired or just to relax. It is an escape at the end of my day, an environment that is both aesthetically exciting as well as healing to my psyche."

*Samuel Botero, Samuel Botero Associates, Inc.*
*150 East 58th Street, 23 Floor, New York, New York 10155*
*Tel.: (212) 935-5155, Fax: (212) 832-0714*

*Photography: Phillip Ennis*

ICE

# *Geoffrey N. Bradfield, ASID*

South African born Geoffrey Bradfield, now a naturalized citizen of the United States, assumed ownership of Jay Spectre, Inc. in 1992. A partner for fifteen years, his creative vigor contributed to the high profile and recognition of the company. Daring and innovative, the company has drawn its inspiration from the Orient, African Primitivism and Art Deco. The company look is rooted in the twentieth century, comfortably streamlined and yet ultra-glamourous. 'Functional opulence' is the key to the company's designs, incorporating fine antiques and high tech, and attaching the same sculptural value to utility objects as to important pieces of art. The results are superbly elegant, intensely comfortable environments that delight the eye, mind and body alike. Mr. Bradfield's published works have appeared in *Architectural Digest, HG, House Beautiful, Metropolitan Home, New York Times* and *Habitat*. He is the co-author of *Point of View Design by Jay Spectre* and author of *Celebration Christmas in New York*. Mr. Bradfield has also been a guest lecturer at The Smithsonian Institution.

"This apartment presented an exciting challenge. Confronted with seven thousand five hundred square feet of raw space, this penthouse in the center of Calgary offers breathtaking views of the city and the distant Canadian Rockies. Our clients, in this instance, are internationally travelled and enjoy a sophisticated lifestyle. The entrance captures the elegant spirit of the open plan living areas. There is a strong architectural reference repeated throughout the apartment. The stepped ceiling, the David Hockney collage, the Jim Dine bronze and the marble and metal inlay floor create a dramatic stage. The dining room repeats the serenity and balance."

*Geoffrey N. Bradfield, ASID, Jay Spectre, Inc.*
*964 Third Avenue, New York, New York 10022*
*Tel.: (212) 758-1773, Fax: (212) 688-1571*

*Photography: H. Durston Saylor*

# *Alfredo Brito*

After living in Europe and Puerto Rico, Cuban-born interior designer Alfredo Brito moved to Florida, becoming a resident in 1973. With a degree in Liberal Arts, his earliest career experience was in Miami with star designer Angelo Donghia. Later, Mr. Brito was affiliated with Burdine's Interior Design Department. In 1985, he opened the design firm bearing his name, which has grown into a full interior design service. Creating interiors ranging from hotels to boats, from offices to window displays, his *forte* is in residential designs. Today, Mr. Brito maintains clients across the United States, Mexico, South America and the Caribbean, gaining international exposure and reputation. Mr. Brito's works have appeared in such prestigious trade publications as *Architectural Digest, Florida Designers of Distinction, Showcase of Interior Design (Southern Edition), Florida's Designers Quarterly,* and in several Latin American and Spanish language magazines and newspapers. As a respected professional in the community, Mr. Brito has been the recipient of numerous awards and has directed several interior design seminars.

"Rooms that reflect exuberance and elegance are what I strive for. A prime example is this living room, located in a ten thousand square foot waterfront residence in Florida. The walls were upholstered in a silk damask and the sofas and chairs were upholstered using a natural color as a background to soften the severe Spanish architecture of the house. A Belgian wool tapestry, a wrought-iron cocktail table and an Indopersian rug tie everything together. On the other side of the room, a *bombée* chest and two lounge chairs create a more intimate setting. For the final touch, a bunch of fresh sunflowers add a splash of vivid color to this luxurious room."

---

*Alfredo Brito, Brito Interior Design, Inc.*
*1000 Quayside Terrace, Suite 412, Miami, Florida 33138*
*Tel.: (305) 895-8539*

*Photography: Dan Forer*

GLORIA NAYLOR

# Ruth Burt

Ruth Burt received her Master's in Painting from New York University, following a B.A. from Marymount Manhattan College. She enhanced her talents for design and color with an Associate Degree from the New York School of Interior Design. Her professional experience includes work with Edward Durell Stone Associates PC, Stuart Mager Inc., Naomi Leff and Associates, Inc., Columbia Pictures Industries, Inc., Mancini•Duffy Associates, and Jack Lenor Larsen, Inc. With a background in both commercial and residential design, Ms. Burt founded her own firm in 1993, specializing in residential design. Ms. Burt believes "faith is the substance of things hoped for, the conviction of things unseen". Hebrews 11:1.

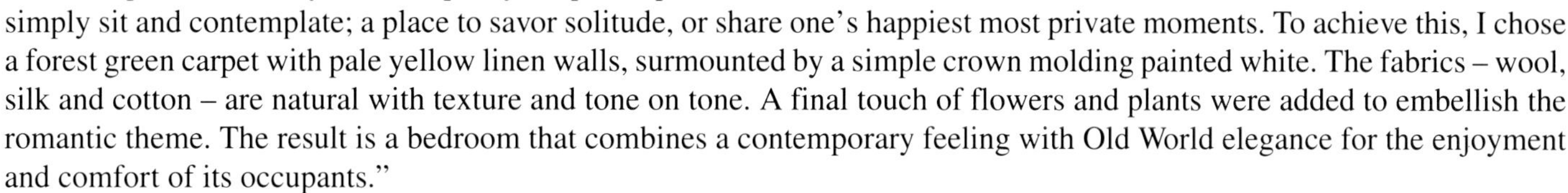

"In the master bedroom of this Fifth Avenue apartment, I have sought to create an atmosphere of beauty and tranquility; a special place in which to rest or read, or simply sit and contemplate; a place to savor solitude, or share one's happiest most private moments. To achieve this, I chose a forest green carpet with pale yellow linen walls, surmounted by a simple crown molding painted white. The fabrics – wool, silk and cotton – are natural with texture and tone on tone. A final touch of flowers and plants were added to embellish the romantic theme. The result is a bedroom that combines a contemporary feeling with Old World elegance for the enjoyment and comfort of its occupants."

*Ruth Burt*
*236 East 82nd Street, Suite 3D, New York, New York 10028*
*Tel.: (212) 737-7507, Fax: (212) 472-7782*

*Photography: Peter Vitale*

# *Barbara Jean Campbell, ASID*

Barbara Campbell, president of her namesake firm, is a Professional Member of the American Society of Interior Designers and has served in offices both locally and nationally. She received her design education in the west at UCLA and her design experience in the east. Serving clients on both coasts has expanded her design knowledge and given her the experience needed to approach each project with a commitment to create environments that are aesthetically pleasing, functional and executed to perfection with special attention to design detail. Ms. Campbell's interiors have appeared in numerous national and regional publications. With a specific interest in barrier free design for the residential environment, she recently authored *Access Washington – A Guide to the Nation's Capitol for the Physically Challenged.*

"Moving from the California Napa Valley to the east coast, my clients wanted to recreate the atmosphere of the Northern California coast in their wine room, which they used for casual entertainment *al fresco*, wine tastings and Sunday brunches. By necessity, the room had to be an interior space, but we wanted to create the feeling of a terrace on the Mediterranean. The walls were *faux* finished to emulate seeping stucco with ivy growing in the cracking exterior. Outdoor furnishings were selected to further create the illusion of an exterior setting. The Luyten Park bench conveys an old world feeling, while the washed tile of the terra cotta floor is decidedly twentieth century. The iron and stone accessories are timeless and add an air of whimsy to the entire setting."

*Barbara Jean Campbell, ASID, Barbara Campbell Interiors*
*9812 Falls Road, Potomac, Maryland 20854*
*Tel.: (301) 983-4255, Fax: (301) 983-8836*

*Photography: Richard K. Robinson*

# *Michael de Santis, ASID*

Michael de Santis is an internationally renowned residential and commercial interior designer. His work appears around the globe – from the United States to the French Riviera to the Middle East. Because of his worldwide recognition, he has participated in numerous design showcase homes, including the prestigious Kips Bay Boys' and Girls' Club Showhouse and the Rogers Memorial Library Showhouse in Southampton. His interiors have graced the covers of *Architectural Digest* and *Interior Design* on numerous occasions, and his work has appeared in all the leading American interior design publications. Past first prize winner of the famous Hexter Award, Mr. de Santis has also received the Award for Excellence in Residential Design at the Chicago Design Fest in Chicago.

"After designing my clients' residence in the northeast, I was commissioned to design their winter residence, located in Palm Beach Gardens, Florida. Due to the location, we opted to create a completely different design concept for this second home. I was able to work on this project from the initial groundbreaking all the way through to final completion, which gave us the opportunity to make any design changes necessary to meet their needs and our concept. While this room is designed in a relaxed contemporary style, I incorporated subtle hints of grandeur to create an aura of substance. The informality of the sofas is balanced by the rich gold tapestry, and a regal air is softly created with the lighted pilasters and the columned floor and table lamps. While somewhat stately in design, these lighting pieces also create a feeling of intimacy within this expansive area, visually lowering the ceiling and bringing the space together, thereby comprising the final elements of this room's design."

*Michael de Santis, ASID, Michael de Santis, Inc.*
*1110 Second Avenue at 58th Street, New York, New York 10022*
*Tel.: (212) 753-8871, Fax: (212) 935-7777*

*Photography: Phillip Ennis*

# Robert Dirstein

A native of Chesley, Ontario, Robert Dirstein completed his education at the Ontario College of Art in 1951. His career as a residential interior designer has now spanned over forty years. For most of that time, since 1956, he has been President of his own independent interior design firm, Dirstein Robertson Limited in Toronto. His major projects include three palaces in Saudi Arabia, as well as commissions in Florida, California, and New York. Mr. Dirstein's work has been published in *Interior Design,* the British edition of *House & Garden,* and *Architectural Digest,* earning the honor of being the only Canadian in its annual 100 Top Designers list.

"As this living room shows, my focus is on traditional design with contemporary comfort. For this living room, I used my client's collection of Sisley and Renoir paintings to serve as a wonderful highlight for the soft celadon background color of the walls and silk draperies. The French floral print of the sofa and two armchairs softens the scheme. I utilized the colors of the sofa fabric – the roses, greens, ivory and gold – and incorporated them into the other furnishings and carpeting. A second matching sofa and armchair ensemble is upholstered in a rich gold material, similar to the silk draperies. A fine mahogany breakfront, circa 1820, in the dining room houses a collection of Derby porcelain. I chose to use mahogany as the main element in the room as seen in the tables, desk and chairs. Large potted plants and colorful floral arrangements complete the setting. I like to think of a room as a painting, and it is my job as the designer to place the elements together to make the composition."

*Robert Dirstein, Dirstein Robertson Limited*
*77 Yorkville Avenue, Toronto, Ontario, Canada M5R 1C1*
*Tel.: (416) 961-6211, Fax: (416) 961-5537*

*Photography: Peter Vitale*

# Trudy Dujardin, ASID

Trudy Dujardin is a multi-award winning interior designer known for residential and commercial interiors, remodeling and historic preservation. A fine artist by talent and undergraduate training, she blends her graduate studies in interior design with her love of people, treating interiors as her canvas. The principal of the full service firm, Trudy Dujardin Interiors of Westport, Connecticut and Nantucket, Massachusetts, she was twice featured on 'Bob Vila's Home Again' (CBS) in 1991. Ms. Dujardin's works have been widely published in national magazines and books. Her designs have appeared on the covers of *Colonial Homes, Decorating Remodeling* and *Good Housekeeping*.

"Two busy professionals sought a very personal retreat on Nantucket Island Shore which would be a comfortable gathering place for family and friends. Careful planning yielded a floorplan which takes advantage of the views of the spectacular harbor and the home's beautiful gardens. A rewarding aspect of this project was its strict adherence to non-toxic and environmentally-sensitive materials dictated by the owners' allergies and concern for the environment. To minimize competition with the natural views, a white textured woven fabric was used throughout the upholstery and window treatments. This serene simplicity is accented with blue, in harmony with the sea, appearing in the nautical and American Impressionist paintings, pillows, trims, antique porcelains, accessories and the foyer's area rug. Custom-made built-ins display the owners' extensive collections, many of which reflect their deep love for the island's history and tradition. In keeping with the nautical theme, the hand-rubbed French patina and custom-milled cherry floors add richness, warmth and a yacht-like atmosphere, while contrasting with the light furniture and sisal carpet. The gracefully curved mezzanine gallery affords an additional water view through the opposite dormer window in the living room's high slanted ceiling. Featuring an antique (c. 1830) ship's piano, the gallery exhibits part of the clients' collection of antique whaling paintings. The room reflects the understated elegance, timelessness and the home's harbor setting, as well as the clients' personalities and interests without sacrificing the comfort and functionality they so much desired."

*Trudy Dujardin, ASID, Trudy Dujardin Interiors*
*3 Sylvan Road South, Westport, Connecticut 06880*
*Tel.: (203) 222-1019; Nantucket, MA Tel.: (508) 228-1120*

*Photography: Jack Weinhold*

STEINWAY & SONS

# *Susanne Eisinger, ASID*

Susanne Eisinger was educated at the University of Maryland, the Corcoran School of Fine Arts in Washington, DC and graduated from the International Institute of Interior Design. In 1980 she founded her firm, Interior Design Concepts, based in Alexandria, Virginia. A Professional Member of the American Society of Interior Designers, Ms. Eisinger's notable works include doctors' suites, law offices, a private hospital and numerous residential projects throughout the eastern United States.

"The living room of this spacious townhouse of Mr. and Mrs. John T. Kane is located in the old town of Alexandria. I used colors mostly in pastels, such as variations of corals in the sponge-paint method on the walls. The furnishings offer a pleasant contrast between light and dark. While the sofa and chairs are upholstered in light beige and tan fabrics, the tables, Oriental screen and grand piano are of dark woods. To enhance the 'old-town' ambience of the city, I kept the wood floors exposed and then placed Oriental rugs throughout the room and entryway. I wanted the final element of this design to please the fanciful tastes of my clients, and we agreed upon a ceiling painted in soft blues and corals, featuring a *trompe l'oeil* effect, complete with cherubs peeking down through the sponge-painted clouds."

*Susanne Eisinger, ASID, Interior Design Concepts*
*P.O. Box 362, Alexandria, Virginia 22313*
*Tel.: (301) 365-7008, Fax: (301) 469-5912*

*Photography: Bill Reeves*

# William R. Eubanks

Memphis, Tennessee is the home of interior designer William Eubanks. Upon completion of his degree in interior design, Mr. Eubanks established his own firm in 1976. His Georgian style showroom is enhanced by fine English and Continental antiques, which for him are natural tools of the trade.

"I chose a warm colorful palette for this drawing room using vivid reds, greens, and yellows against subtle ochre-glazed paneled walls. Chinese porcelain and stone figures, fine English and Continental antiques and accessories, down-filled upholstery, and fringed draperies flanking Palladian windows give this room a comfortable yet timeless old world quality."

*William R. Eubanks, William R. Eubanks Interior Design*
*1516 Union Avenue, Memphis, Tennessee 38104*
*Tel.: (901) 272-1825, Fax: (901) 272-1845*

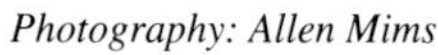

*Photography: Allen Mims*

ENGLISH FURNITURE
THE ENGLISH DOG at Home
PORCELAIN for PALACES
GARDENS OF THE NATIONAL TRUST

# *Elwyn Colby Ferris*

With an interior design career that spans nearly twenty years, Elwyn Colby Ferris founded his own firm in Washington DC in 1986 after training with the prestigious design firm of Trade Winds in his hometown of Boston. Firmly rooted in tradition, but reinterpreted for today's contemporary tastes, Mr. Ferris' award winning interiors have been featured in numerous publications, including the *Boston Globe, House and Garden, House Beautiful* and *Interior Visions*. A member of the National Trust for Historic Preservation, he has been a participating designer for the Boston Junior League Decorator Showhouse and the Baltimore Symphony Decorators' Showhouse.

"The first rays of sunshine reveal a fresh and airy space that becomes romantically dramatic by nightfall. A custom designed neoclassic mantle with a mirrored surround covers an unattractive black Victorian fireplace, and gives the space needed architectural strength. The walls are glazed in a subtle cross-stitch pattern, and finished to resemble fine Celadon porcelain. The cherry floors were refinished and left bare. An abundance of creamy-white Belgian linen covers nearly everything. The linen is handpainted in a stylized trellis pattern for the bed coverlet as a compliment to the rose and lilac print lining the bed canopy. The striking, polished aluminum Athena chairs and the silver-leafed drapery poles and screen introduce a myriad of silver-finished surfaces from sterling to mercury glass that punctuate and lend sparkle to this serene and comfortable bedroom."

*Elwyn Colby Ferris, Elwyn Colby Ferris Interior Design*
*1417 T Street, NW, Washington DC 20009*
*Tel.: (202) 387-3161, Fax: (202) 332-8804*

*Photography: Timothy Fields (large room photo)*

# *Landy Gardner*

Landy Gardner, of Landy Gardner Interiors, based in Nashville, Tennessee, specializes in residential and office interior design and decoration. Mr. Gardner's work is featured in *Showcase of Interior Design, Southern Accents, Traditional Homes, Southern Living,* and *Nashville* magazine, which named him Designer of the Year.

"When the owners of this classic Italianate home decided to add an additional room to their residence, they wanted a very large space to incorporate the exterior landscape. The room needed to facilitate large meetings, social gatherings of one hundred or more guests, and sit-down family dinners for thirty, yet provide intimate ambience and perfect comfort for two. The glass walls and a glass ceiling created a marvelous open solarium aura. The furnishings and accessories were collected from England, New York, and Nashville, and then integrated with favorite family pieces. The completed room exudes a unique charm – special in style, yet still classic; spacious, yet still warm and inviting."

*Landy Gardner, Landy Gardner Interiors*
*1903 21st Avenue South, Nashville, Tennessee 37212*
*Tel.: (615) 383-1880, Fax: (615) 383-4167*

*Photography: Jonathan Hillyer*

# Chip Johnston, ASID

Residential projects are the focus of Chip Johnston's Atlanta-based interior design firm. Educated at Emory University and University of North Carolina at Chapel Hill, Mr. Johnston gained valuable interior design experience in a variety of positions before opening his own firm in 1979. As a Professional Member of the American Society of Interior Designers, he has received a number of accolades from his peers, including an Industry Foundation Citation, a Medalist Award and three Presidential Citations. His memberships in the National Trust for Historic Preservation, Cooper-Hewitt Museum and several fine arts organizations speak highly of his commitment to a professional, cultured approach to every project.

"Three shuttered Palladian windows fronting this gracious living room shed filtered light on plants, flowers, porcelains, antique woods and handsome fabrics into this captivating space. The subtle gleam of old leather in the English screen and the soft patination of the French elm table are underscored by the corals and ivory of the English-bordered rug. The color scheme, a bright mix of coral, green, gold, ivory and blue, is visible in each element of the design, with each piece complementing and accenting the others. A hint of peach tints the walls, highlighting the rug and the large floral painting above the cushioned comfort of the celadon sofa. Brightness is added by the 'peony vine' of the Chippendale couch, the silky plaid table skirting, and the stripe applied to the antique mahogany chair, creating a warm, inviting and charming space."

*Charles "Chip" A. Johnston, Jr., ASID, IFDA, Chip Johnston Interiors*
*2996 Grandview Avenue N.E., Suite 300, Atlanta, Georgia 30305*
*Tel.: (404) 231-4141, Fax: (404) 261-3713*

*Photography: David S. Schilling*

# Judith Sisler Johnston

After receiving her Bachelor of Arts degree from Keane College, Judith Sisler Johnston obtained her Master's degree from Northeast Missouri State University in 1972. Currently, Ms. Johnston serves as president of Sisler-Williams Interior Design in Jacksonville, which opened in 1985. A multifaceted designer, she has been recognized with interior design awards in the health care, country club, residential and model home categories. With the design team comprised of partner Rita T. Williams and Colleen Phillips, they completed the interior design of this model showhome featured here.

"The living room of this model showhome in Stuart, Florida combines contemporary style with neoclassical design. Our main objective was to highlight the beauty of the home and its surrounding areas, so we chose to pay particular attention to the pool and grounds by minimizing the window treatments. With its soft taupe background, seen in the draperies and walls, the sofa and matching armchair lend themselves to the elegance of the room. Simple neoclassical furnishings, such as the floor lamp, coffee table and vase, add to the charm of this room. The dining room, entry gallery and library feature washed maple woods, skirted side chairs and black-lacquer tapestry host chairs, formal window treatments and neoclassical decorative lighting."

*Judith Sisler Johnston, Sisler-Williams Interior Design*
*9143 Phillips Highway, Suite 260, Jacksonville, Florida 32256*
*Tel.: (904) 363-0177, Fax: (904) 363-9980*

*Photography: Everett & Soulé*

# Debra S. Kelley

With clients throughout the United States, Debra Kelley has specialized in both commercial and residential interior design during her fourteen-year career. Since 1986, she has owned and operated her own interior design firm, Kelley Designs, which has a staff of six designers. An Associate Member of the International Society of Interior Designers, Ms. Kelley has received numerous awards and recognition. For the past three years, she has been featured in *Who's Who in Interior Design*. Ms. Kelley recently completed a restaurant project at the world-famous Kaanapali Golf Resort on Maui, and her firm is currently working on projects in Florida and New York.

"My clients wanted this oceanfront second home on Hilton Head Island to be an elegant getaway for their family. The volume of this living room, with its twenty-foot ceilings, presented a real challenge to provide an intimate, casual warmth to a room with such strong architectural features. In contrast to their permanent residence in Pennsylvania, we worked with a soft palette of colors more suited to the Island look. Light greens, fushias, pinks and cremes were used in the furnishings, while dark colors dominate the accessories. To bring the dramatic oceanfront views indoors, I kept the window treatments light and to a minimum using soft, subtle colors and fabrics.

"While the bold architectural statements of the sixteen-inch plaster crown moldings, columns, capitals and the two-story segmented bay windows create a feeling of grandeur, I employed custom over-stuffed furnishings and unique accessories to give the room a more human scale."

*Debra S. Kelley, Kelley Designs, Inc.*
*30 New Orleans Road, Hilton Head Island, South Carolina 29928*
*Tel.: (803) 785-6911, Fax: (803) 785-6778*

*Photography: Skip Meachen*

# Patricia A. Lazor, Allied ASID

Patricia A. Lazor received her Bachelor of Arts Degree from Chestnut Hill College and later studied at Parsons School of Design and the New York School of Interior Design. She has been designing both residential and contract spaces for the past twenty years. Patricia A. Lazor is known for having a clever design sense when mixing a rich palette of colors and textures in her rooms, and her rooms always reflect quiet elegance. Although she has a penchant for antiques, her own custom-designed furniture is often incorporated in her interiors. Her design range is broad; she has delighted children with her whimsical bedrooms and has pleased owners of country homes with her comfortable, sophisticated style. Her contemporary designs also display her diverse design skills.

"This library was designed as a relaxing space for a family to congregate comfortably, yet it possesses enough richness for entertaining on a more formal scale. The room already had the bold wood details, dating from the early 1900's, when the designer began working on the room. These strong details provide a splendid backdrop to a room that is filled with family treasures. The room recalls several generations of family, past and present, with custom designed furniture as well as antique furniture, art, books and accessories selected by the designer from all over the world."

*Patricia A. Lazor, Patricia Lazor, Inc.*
*Roebling Road, Bernardsville, New Jersey 07924*
*Tel.: (908) 766-4019, Fax: (908) 766-7610*

*Photography: John Parsekian*

# Michael Love, ASID

For thirty years, Michael Love has been applying her design skills not just to interiors, but also for the public good and to educate others in her industry. Since founding Quantum Design Group in 1970, Ms. Love has completed major contract, residential and space management projects in the United States, Africa, Asia and Europe. The range of her abilities is indicated by the description of several projects: the offices for Avatar Investors/Zweig Group, the East Hampton Inn lobby, and the one thousand seat Cultural Center in Calabar, Nigeria. Ms. Love was the design consultant for all non-tenant spaces in the New York World Trade Center when it was built.

"Located in a New York City brownstone, this living room was designed to fulfill my clients' desire to create a spacious and modern interior from five existing small rooms. The stainless steel fireplace facade was custom designed to develop a center of interest in the living room area, and to balance the clients' collection of Eskimo sculpture and Indian paintings. I especially love the creation of a stylized river flowing through the area rug. This rug was designed to create movement on the floor and visually bring together the various areas of the room, which were very rectilinear. The cohesive element of this design is the color palette of creme, navy, bone and terra cotta, which have always been my favorite background colorings. This palette takes us away from the stark white, while the navy is softer than black as an accent, and lends a perfect final element to this room's design."

*Michael Love, ASID, Quantum Design Group*
*121 Madison Avenue, New York, New York 10016*
*Tel.: (212) 545-0301, Fax: (212) 689-4064*

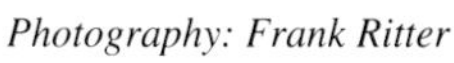

*Photography: Frank Ritter*

# *Emma Matienzo-Smeal*

Emma Smeal's international design work has been earning her merit for over twenty-five years. Her expertise is finding *objets d'art* and devising color and lighting techniques. In addition to interior design, Ms. Smeal's educational attainment includes fine arts and psychology. She attended the Karilagan Finishing School in Manila, the Ateneo de Manila Business School and the Inchbald School in London. Ms. Smeal is an Allied Member of the American Society of Interior Designers and a Design Associate for the National Trust for Historic Preservation.

"When they retained me, my clients were recovering from an unsuccessful attempt at decorating their house. They stressed that a European look was what they wanted. I scoured some pieces from New York art dealers, but most of my lucky finds were at la Porte de Clignancourt in France. The *Finis Corona* is an 1876 *trumeau* graced on both sides by Marie Theresa crystal sconces. The credenza placed beneath the *trumeau* is a Louis XV reproduction and the area rug is a French needlepoint. The chairs were done with twenty-four karat gold leaf and the fabric used was custom-made tapestry. The timeless quality found in rich European design gives this room an ornate feeling, without being excessive."

*Emma Matienzo-Smeal, Allied ASID, E.S.C./A.A. Decor, The Design Group of Washington*
*4020 Biscayne Dr., Winter Springs, Florida 32708* *10108 Springlake Dr., Fairfax, Virginia 22030*
*Tel.: (407) 695-2500, Fax: (407) 366-3324* *Tel.: (703) 273-4466*

*Photography: Mark Dolan*

# *Rod Maxwell, ISID*

The work of interior designer Rod Maxwell has often been described by the press and his peers as 'painterly'. Mr. Maxwell's interiors reflect his artist's background, as he considers the aesthetics of the spaces he designs. "Since design is a visual art, vignettes and room designs must be viewed as a painter would construct a still-life to be painted," Mr. Maxwell explains. "All elements of rhythm, motif, contrasting forms, focus, balance, positive and negative space, and color should be considered. The completed design is one in which all the integral parts work together to create the whole."

After receiving his Fine Arts degree from Rockford College, Mr. Maxwell began his career in the floral and commercial design fields. When display clients requested Mr. Maxwell's help with their homes, he made a full transition from display to interior design, opening R.A. Maxwell, Inc. in 1980. He was immediately recognized by the Merchandise Mart and Chicago Design Sources as a 'Star on the Horizon,' and since, has garnered more awards and national design features. In 1991, Mr. Maxwell was named the Designer of the Year by *Midwest Living Magazine*, and received its Design Excellence Award. Mr. Maxwell has served on the Board of the International Society of Interior Designers and on the Merchandise Mart Advisory Board. He lectures extensively, and has participated in numerous design showhouses throughout the Chicago area, including the Merchandise Mart, the Hinsdale Decorator's Showcase, the Park Ridge Youth Campus Designers' Showhouse and the ORT Decorator's Showcase. Mr. Maxwell's works have been published in numerous magazines including *Better Homes and Gardens, Midwest Living* and *North Shore Home & Decor*. Also, he has had feature profiles written about him in the *Chicago Tribune*, the *Chicago Sun-Times, Chicago, North Shore, The Daily Herald* and *Furniture Today*.

"This updated Victorian home contains all the details and charm of a vintage home with the advantages of a new one. The home is designed in a Carpenter Gothic style. For the second floor guest room, the shape and size of the room presented several challenges in designing an inviting and comfortable space that reflects the home's character and style. A Victoria & Albert reproduction wallcovering, one of my favorites, softens the edges of this octagon-shaped room. Amid the lush cabbage rose bouquets are silhouettes of the Royal Highnesses defined in the streaming tendrils. The ground color of the wallcovering is a rich antique ecru, which appears to have aged gently over the years. The glossy trim and baseboard enamel was specially tinted to give a softened 'been there forever' look. I chose a daybed for its versatility. It gives the advantage of seating, as well as sleeping. Throw pillows of the same cabbage rose design rest upon the bed and two plush, oversized chairs. The natural sisal carpeting was installed wall to wall and overlaid with an overscaled rose-bouquet patterned needlepoint rug. Romantic lace curtains soften the daylight through floor-to-ceiling windows. Pillows trimmed with antique buttons, elegant green opaline lustres and fine blue and white porcelain complete the ambience. The adjoining bath and hallway are treated with the same wallcovering to soften the edges and create a cozy unified retreat."

---

*Rod Maxwell, ISID, R.A. Maxwell, Inc.*
*5461 N. East River Road, Suite 901, Chicago, Illinois 60656-1130*
*Tel.: (312) 693-2857, Fax: (312) 693-6620*

*Photography: Steve Donisch*

# *H. Glenn McGee, AIA, ASID*

A native of South Carolina, Glenn McGee graduated from Clemson University with a Bachelor of Architecture degree. His thirty-year career has spanned seven states and includes travel and study in Italy, Switzerland, Austria, Canada, the Bahamas and Saudi Arabia. A member of both the AIA and the ASID, Mr. McGee's office is now in Florida, where he specializes in custom residential design work. In addition to his prestigious career as a designer, Mr. McGee has been active as a lecturer on Interior Design and Architectural History at the University of South Carolina.

"Located in northeast Chattanooga, this great room overlooks the peaceful duck-filled lagoon of Wolftever Creek. This large area had to serve the functions of dining, entertainment and as the centerpoint for circulation to surrounding spaces and another floor. My client wanted a room that was comfortable and relaxing. The two-story space is dominated by a magnificent fireplace of native Tennessee stone and the antique *farahan* serapi was selected to share the focal point and be the inspiration for our fabric color palette. The walls are cypress wood, which has been brushed in off-white paint, cloth-rubbed to show the wood grain, and then flat glazed. This light beige colored, sun-filled envelope became the surface to display the owners' collection of art works. Furniture wood colors were selected to be light, with accents of black in accessory items. The heart pine wood floor has been stained a honey color which displays the Persian rugs and pulls this surface together, so that it becomes the base for our furniture. Accessories, so very important in any design, were carefully selected and minimized. The end result has pleased our client and produced a project in which I take great pride."

*H. Glenn McGee, AIA, ASID, McGee-Howle & Associates, Architects, Inc.*
*2801 Ocean Drive, Suite 302, Vero Beach, Florida 32963*
*Tel.: (407) 231-4222, Fax: (407) 231-4311*

*Photography: Jim Madden*

# Carol Meltzer, ASID

Carol Meltzer studied liberal arts at the F.I.T. School of Interior Design in New York City. She began her career as an interior designer with Nishho-Iwai and is currently president of P.T.M. Interiors Unlimited Designs, Inc. in New York City. An allied member of the New York Metropolitan Chapter of the American Society of Interior Designers, Ms. Meltzer is also a member of the American Center for Design. Her projects have been published in the *New York Post*, the *New York Times* and numerous magazines. Her design style focuses on each client's personal needs, space and lifestyle. Along with the interior design, Ms. Meltzer also creates interior decorations to complement each room. She incorporates past traditions with current environmental concerns to create an aesthetic balance.

"I believe design is a reflection of life and I am constantly developing new services and products to meet the needs of my clients. Combining soft tones in the furnishings and accessories, I have achieved an atmosphere that is both warm and inviting for this penthouse living room, located in New York City. The plush light beige sofas match the adjoining dining room chairs and the custom carpet. A custom designed, 'star light' mirrored ceiling adds to the illusion of living room's expanse, casting a warm glow throughout the space."

*Carol Meltzer, ASID, P.T.M. Interiors Unlimited Designs, Inc.*
*107 East 60th Street, New York, New York 10022*
*Tel.: (212) 688-4430, Fax: (212) 688-4463*
*64345 Via Risso, Palm Springs, California 92262*
*Tel.: (619) 322-6084, Fax: (619) 322-6084*

*Photography: James Levin*

MARY C. HENDERSON
ABRAMS
THEATER IN AMERICA

# Noranit Tui Pranich, ASID

Noranit Tui Pranich, principal of Pranich & Associates, holds a professional degree in architecture from Cornell University. His background includes both residential and commercial interior and architectural designs. Pranich & Associates is noted for its fresh and exciting design concepts and its end-to-end capabilities. Mr. Pranich maintains his philosophy of high design standards and keeps a watchful eye on healthy controlled growth for the firm.

Mr. Pranich's experience ranges from working with prominent residential and commercial interior design firms in Los Angeles and New York to involvement with a well established Palm Beach architectural firm. Since 1984, his work has encompassed residential and commercial installations in Palm Beach, Wellington, Boca Raton, Miami and New York. Mr. Pranich is recognized and published in national and international magazines such as *Thai House and Garden, Elle, Palm Beach Life, Southern Accents* and *Palm Beach Illustrated.* A licensed interior designer, Mr. Pranich serves as a board member of American Society of Interior Designers.

"The living room area, located in a home in Palm Beach, Florida, is decorated in a light and sophisticated style. I used several textures of fabric and leather along with different earth tones to give the room a warm look. The furnishings are a diverse collection of antiques, mixed with an Oriental bench, chair and an iron coffee table. The rooms are accented with Oriental accessories to give an eclectic and 'lived-in' feel."

*Noranit Tui Pranich, ASID, Pranich & Associates*
*270 South County Road, Palm Beach, Florida 33480*
*Tel.: (407) 655-1192, Fax: (407) 655-2106*

*Photography: Dan Forer*

# *Sandi Samole, ASID, IDG*

In 1979, Sandi Samole founded S & B Interiors Inc., a design firm specializing in residential and corporate office design. A graduate of De Paul University in Chicago, her projects range from modern to Country French. Ms. Samole's works have been published in numerous magazines, and recently she was honored with the cover story in *Interiors and Sources*. A respected lecturer and author, her topics have ranged from 'How Designers and Manufacturers Can Work Together', to 'How to Work with an Interior Designer' to 'Contracts and Running an Interior Design Business'.

"It was my desire to do these spaces with an eye towards making all pieces a 'work of art'. To maintain a feeling of warmth, traditionally styled sofas and chairs were used, but finished in high gloss black lacquer for a more modern feeling. Since the dining room was to be used on a regular basis, granite was chosen for the table top, and was air-brushed with color and then treated with polyurethane. The accessories selected ranged from newly created glass sculptures to antique plates that had been in the family for years, thus completing the desire for a 'transitional' look."

*Sandi Samole, ASID, IDG, S & B Interiors, Inc., Fl. Lic. 1B00000056*
*9700 Dixie Highway, Suite 1030, Miami, Florida 33156*
*Tel.: (305) 670-4148, 661-1577, Fax: (305) 661-2722*

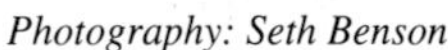

*Photography: Seth Benson*

# Darryl Savage

Darryl Savage was born in Washington, DC and educated at the New School for Social Research in New York. During his design career, he has completed residential and commercial projects throughout the Mid-Atlantic region, and has won numerous awards for his work. As president and principal designer of DHS Designs, Inc., located in Annapolis, Maryland, Mr. Savage's work speaks of classicism and warmth, clean lines and rich textures.

"I wanted to create a romantic retreat – in the mood of a relaxed gentility – devoid of sharp contrasts. To achieve this, I employed a neutral palette, the play of shades from white to creme. Interest is derived through texture: stone, damask, antique crystal and lace, dried boxwood and aged gilt. A signature Baltimore marble mantle, neoclassical crystal chandelier, terra cotta finials, English carved and painted wooden desk, and bronze chenets are among the antiques that lend an aura of old world comfort to this bedroom. Overcoming such obstacles as a cavernous cathedral ceiling and an odd assortment of windows, the resulting effect of warmth and character is at once ethereal and elegant."

*Darryl H. Savage, DHS Designs, Inc.*
*86 Maryland Avenue, Annapolis, Maryland 21401*
*Tel.: (410) 280-3466, Fax: (410) 647-6816*

*Photography: Anne Gummerson*

# Patricia S. Stotler

Born, raised and educated in Pennsylvania, Pat Stotler obtained her Master's degree from Syracuse University just prior to moving to Florida in 1968. Since 1980, she has been the owner and principal designer of her own firm. Her philosophy and style incorporate her clients' personal collections of furnishings and accessories into each design. Ms. Stotler's projects include homes found in country club communities, oceanfront condominiums, as well as lavish custom homes.

"For this winter residence my clients (the husband, a builder, and the wife, an architect) wanted their house to have the finished look of a model home, with everything inside beautifully coordinated. Our mission was to create a very livable and comfortable residence suitable for guests of all ages, using the wife's favorite colors of teals and roses in many shades. The end tables are Oriental hand-painted boxes and the glass cocktail table base is made of stone. An original commissioned oil painting by Judith Weidman highlights the bright colors of the room. A second original piece by the same artist serves as the centerpiece of the adjoining dining room. For this space, proportion was very important as floor space is limited, even though the high ceiling creates much volume visually. To make the room appear symmetrical, a Hart chandelier with textured shades and crystal baubles is hung low above the table, while tall brass candlesticks are placed on the table. The pinstripe fabric used on the chairs is repeated in the drapery treatment and the brightly colored Indo Serapi Oriental rug contains virtually all the colors used throughout the residence."

*Patricia S. Stotler, Pat Stotler Interiors, Inc.*
*110 Coral Cay Drive, BallenIsles, Palm Beach Gardens, Florida 33418*
*Tel.: (407) 627-0527, Fax: (407) 626-7015*

*Photography: Kim Sargent*

# Vicki Wenger, ASID

Principal designer and president of Beautiful Spaces Inc., Vicki Wenger also presides over Vicki Wenger Interiors. Producer and host of *Design Edition*, her own cable TV show, Mrs. Wenger has made television appearances on *Good Morning Washington* and the *Carole Randolph Show*. Her works have been published locally and nationally in *The Washington Post, The Washington Star, Interiors Magazine, Interior Design Magazine* and *1001 Home Ideas*. Ms. Wenger has been an active participant in ASID, and is a past National Board member and past President of the Maryland Chapter.

"This elegant mansion in Washington DC was the scene of many gala evenings and elegant *soirées*. In the stair hall, we are re-living those fabulous parties. I realized that the hall's function was not only to get from one floor to the next, but to get there in style. The ornate wrought iron staircase brings the host and hostess to their many guests below. The beautiful block-painted walls and magnificently accented ceiling serve as an elegant backdrop to the fine furnishings in this room. Understated and elegant, each piece of furniture or *objet d'art*, from the white marble 19th century Italian statue to the eight panel Coromandel screen to the *Le Smoking* series of paintings by Chryssa, was carefully selected to enhance the beauty of this space. The end result is an eclectic mix of past and present."

*Vicki Wenger, ASID, Beautiful Spaces, Inc.*
*2801 New Mexico Avenue, NW, Washington DC, 20007*
*Tel.: (202) 337-4463, Fax: (202) 298-8216*

*Photography: Gordon Beall (room); Kaplan Photography (portrait)*

# Vicente Wolf

In the world of contemporary design, Vicente Wolf has been at the top for over twenty years. Under Vicente Wolf Associates, Inc., he designed such diversified projects as Mrs. Yul Brynner's New York residence, a store in Hong Kong, a New York office building lobby, the 1990 Kips Bay Showhouse, and the Andrew Fezza Company's offices and showrooms.

In addition to major decoration projects, Mr. Wolf designed a furniture collection for Henredon Furniture Industries. The Vicente Wolf Collection includes upholstered furniture as well as a line of slipcovers for their Natchez Collection. The Cuban designer also designed a flatware collection for Sasaki, a table top line for the L.S. Collection, and upholstery fabric for Toltec Fabrics.

"Richland, in Natchez, Mississippi, was built in 1843 and through the years has maintained its original integrity with its Greek revival simplicity and strength. It stands as a Southern plantation style jewel. My greatest challenge was to create an environment which represented my client's modern style of living while still staying in tune with the house's origins. My contemporary classic style blended perfectly with that of the house. My strong feeling is that a traditional piece of furniture or home cannot be locked in its past. In order for it to stay alive, it must evolve with the times."

*Vicente Wolf, Vicente Wolf Associates, Inc.*
*333 West 39 Street, New York, New York 10018*
*Tel.: (212) 465-0590, Fax: (212) 465-0639*

*Photography: Langdon Clay (room), James Hughes (portrait)*

# NORTH AMERICA: WEST

***Jack Adams, ASID,*** Living Room/Entry, Penthouse Condominium

***Nancy J. Anderson, ASID,*** Traditional Bedroom, San Francisco

***Kathleen Buoymaster,*** Traditional Living Room, La Jolla

***Lillian Chain, ASID,*** English Tudor Living Room, Los Angeles

***Cordelia Cortés,*** Cortijo Ranch House, Mexico

***Rodger Dobbel, ASID,*** Country Retreat, San Francisco Bay Area

***Juan Jose Espiñeira,*** Penthouse Living Room/Dining Room, Acapulco Bay

***Kim E. Gwozdz,*** Contemporary Study, Phoenix

***Anthony Jules Harris,*** Contemporary Living/Dining Room, Mexico City

***Myriel Hiner,*** Art Deco Living Room, Omaha

***Patricia Klee, ASID,*** Trophy Room-Entry Area/Stable Complex, Santa Ynez

***Pat Larin, ASID,*** Contemporary Kitchen/Dining Room, Northern California

***Cynthia S. Leftwich, ASID, IBD,*** Southwest Family Room, Texas

***Lois E. Lugonja, ASID,*** Grand Drawing Room, Los Altos Hills

***Gloria Roberts, ISID,*** Guest Sitting Room, Riverside

***Barbara Marie Sande,*** Country Living Room, Lafayette

***Mary L. Sorenson,*** Contemporary Kitchen, Texas

***James Steinmeyer, ISID, ASID, CINOA,*** Traditional Master Bedroom, Texas

***Edward Turrentine, ASID,*** Traditional Living Room, Pasadena

***Ron Wilson,*** Grand Master Bedroom Suite, Beverly Hills

***Susan A. Wolfe, ISID,*** Traditional Living/Dining Room, Mexico City

***Bettye Jordan Young,*** Grand Traditional Living Room

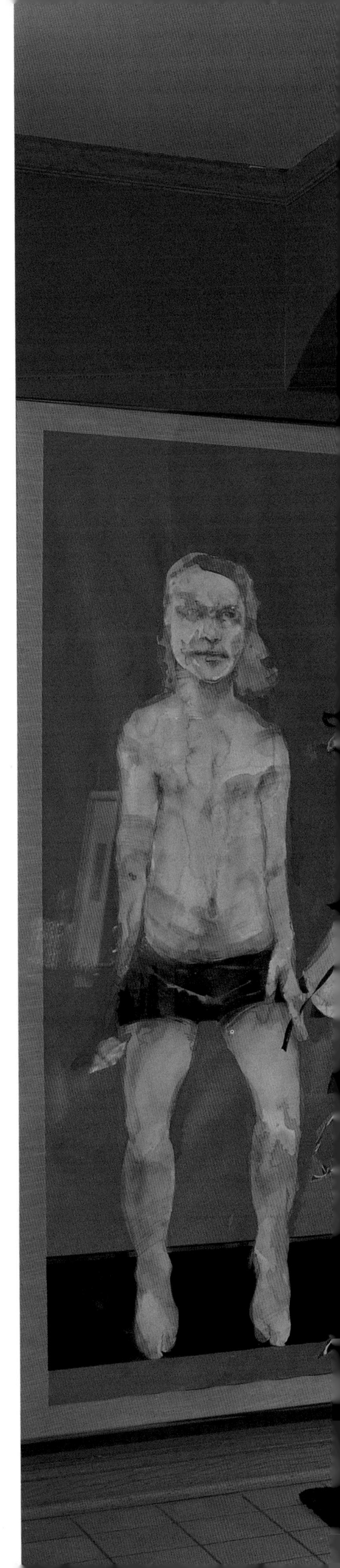

*A visual assault of bright red stimulates the senses, while the large painting, unique console table and handcrafted brass stair rail complete this striking foyer. Interior design: Myrial Hiner, Allied ASID. Photography: Andrew Baran.*

# Jack Adams, ASID

Born in Abilene, Texas, Jack Adams received his Bachelor's degree from West Point, a B.A. from the Art Center College of Design, and did postgraduate work at a number of other schools and universities. He was a project designer for Richard Crowell Associates for three years, and then worked as director of interior design for Media 5 Architects, and interior designer and marketing director for Dale Keller & Associates. Since 1977, Mr. Adams has been principal designer and president of Adams Design, Inc., in Honolulu. His projects include the Mauna Kea Villas, the Sheraton Princeton in Kauai, the lobby of the Bank of Honolulu, The Punahou Cliffs, The Queen Victoria, and the public areas of the forty-story Park Place condominium in Atlanta, Georgia. Mr. Adams is a Professional Member of the American Society of Interior Designers, and his work has been featured in numerous design-related publications, most recently in *Island Home Magazine*.

"This penthouse condominium, located forty floors above the city of Atlanta, provided a rare opportunity to create a unique architectural ambience in a loft space with a sixteen-foot ceiling. At my client's request, I designed massive arches to frame the space. I was asked to meld their existing antique furniture with a contemporary post-modern environment. To achieve this, we evolved a style based on the Biedermeier influence of the 1830's in Austria. Custom cabinetry as well as custom door frames and built-in details reflected this feeling. In addition to the dramatic height, I was able to enhance the feeling of spaciousness by the use of mirrors at the end of the living and dining room area to echo the arches and columns. The overall effect is one of subdued grandeur."

*Jack Adams, ASID, Adams Design, Inc.*
*1415 Kalakaua Avenue, Suite 204, Honolulu, Hawaii 96826*
*Tel.: (808) 955-6100, Fax: (808) 947-4311*

# Nancy J. Anderson, ASID

Since the start of her interior design career, Nancy Anderson has been designing residences and offices for a myriad of clients throughout the United States and Puerto Rico. She received her Bachelor of Arts degree in interior design from Michigan State University, and obtained her advanced study at Parsons School of Design in New York. Ms. Anderson began her career at W.J. Sloanes' New York City store. She later transferred to the company's San Francisco office and gained more design experience on the west coast before opening her own interior design office in the San Francisco Bay area. While working for Sloanes, a major nationwide design company, Ms. Anderson gained experience working for many different clients with very different needs and styles. Her trademark and philosophy is that each client is individual, special, and has a very distinct style. In many instances, clients cannot articulate what they want, but by appreciating the style and feeling of their existing furnishings, Ms. Anderson is able to develop and enhance that special uniqueness that is just right for each client's home. After living in New York, Chicago and San Francisco, she understands that there is a uniqueness which exists within each area and locality. Styles that would be appropriate for New York would not necessarily apply to San Francisco, for example, and would not properly express the taste of those whom live in those locations.

A Professional Member of the American Society of Interior Designers in San Francisco, Ms. Anderson has contributed to numerous society functions and has served on ASID committees. She has a great interest in antiques and has a particular appreciation for objects that can add special meaning and substance to a room's design. Her moto is "individuality, individuality, individuality."

"This particular client has an extensive interest in early California art, animals and subjects pertaining to nature. While designing many of the rooms in this Bay area home, I was able to incorporate her interests into the decor of various rooms throughout the house. For this master bedroom, we started with the headboard, which was an existing piece which my client wanted to showcase. Using this charming handcarved headboard as a centerpiece, we began the entire design of the bedroom around this key element. I then started searching for unusual accent pieces, and first located a wonderful antique wicker chair and commissioned to have it reupholstered to blend with the colors and textures that developed within the room. The two sets of antique African *kuba* cloth, originally used for ceremonial skirts, were hung from tree twigs to create an unusual and striking wall tapestry. Each rectangular bit of cloth, in the traditional native colors of brown and camel, is hand woven from cotton and linen. The custom shutters were painted in a subtle off-white hue, and installed in such a way that they are hinged at the top as to open downward, thereby giving the room a more tropical and natural feeling. Other doors in the room were replaced with matching shutter doors, accentuating the window treatment and carrying through the same tropical impression. The design is completed with various accent pieces, all in the same soft palette of earth colors, made up of beige, tan, burgundy and terra cotta. These colors bring each separate element of this room together, completing this warm, inviting and cozy space."

*Nancy J. Anderson, ASID, Nancy J. Anderson Interiors*
*3065 Clay Street, San Francisco, California 94115*
*Tel.: (415) 346-5022, (800) 484-9971 x5022, Fax: (415) 346-1554*

*Photography: John Vaughan*

# *Kathleen Buoymaster*

A graduate of Duke University and the Interior Designers' Guild of Los Angeles, Kathleen Buoymaster previously was a senior designer for the prestigious firm of Cannell and Chaffin before she founded Kathleen Buoymaster, Inc. in La Jolla, California in 1985. By 1990, she had expanded her design firm to include a boutique showroom which displays and features, in beautiful vignettes, custom furnishings and accessories she's collected from around the world. Her design assignments include domestic as well as international projects. As president of Kathleen Buoymaster, Inc. Interior Design and Design Boutique, she has a staff of five and comments about her business "it is my passion."

"This project was designed to present a feeling of warm formality. It is a room full of beauty and graciousness which reflects my clients' tastes and lifestyle. An old world mix of European style furnishings and rich fabrics was selected for this French influenced architectural statement. A good marriage between the architecture and the interiors is a must for good design. Entertaining was also an important factor for these clients as we planned the furniture placement, providing many conversational groupings. Colors are warm and dramatic, but always classic."

*Kathleen Buoymaster, Kathleen Buoymaster Inc.*
*6933 La Jolla Boulevard, La Jolla, California 92037*
*Tel.: (619) 456-2850, Fax: (619) 456-0672*

*Photography: Edward Gohlich*

# *Lillian Chain, ASID*

Lillian Chain, a National Director of ASID, has a talent for making her decorative skills seem effortless. A native of Los Angeles, she founded Carson-Chain Interiors in 1965. Her client list reads like a Who's Who in the entertainment industry and the interiors she has created for film and TV personalities have won numerous accolades and awards. Her work has been published in many prestigious magazines such as *Architectural Digest* and *House Beautiful*. The outstanding Vera's Retreat in the Glen was profiled on *Lifestyles of the Rich and Famous*. Her community involvement in Los Angeles is legendary, encompassing many outreach programs, all of which have brought a full range of experience and maturity to her work.

"This English Tudor residence is owned by an accomplished sculptress whose works are displayed with a grand collection of antique *cloisonné*, all of which had to coexist harmoniously. The color palette of peach, salmon, bronze and teal create a background for custom furnishings, custom cabinetry and sensitive lighting. The focus on the antique Oriental lacquer screen sets the theme for accents in the dining area."

*Lillian Chain, ASID, Carson-Chain Interiors*
*2222 Ave. of the Stars, Suite 2501, Los Angeles, California 90067*
*Tel.: (310) 277-3855, Fax: (310) 203-8603*

*Photography: Mary E. Nichols*

# Cordelia Cortés

Throughout her twenty-year career, Cordelia Cortés has garnered prominent respect from her clients and peers for her innovative interior design style. Many clients, including architectural industry executives in Mexico, describe her style as "state of the art". Ms. Cortés has showcased her exclusive style in many of her projects, including various commercial and residential designs throughout her native Mexico and the United States. Her unique imagination, ability and skills, described as both classic and modern, have granted Ms. Cortés the distinguished appreciation from even the strictest interior design critics.

"One of my latest creations is this *cortijo*, a ranch-style house complete with a full-sized bullring. Owned by a world renowned horseback bullfighter, I took his love of the sport and incorporated it into the design of the spacious living room. Large chandeliers made of bull-horns are mixed with a combination of spotlights and halogen lights, while the wood walls and ceilings were left bare to enhance the rustic charm of the room. The furnishings are arranged to provide three separate seating areas – the wood dining set at the far wall, the wood benches and chairs at the near wall, and the more luxurious seating of the large armchairs and sofa facing the fireplace. The focal point of the room is the stone fireplace with one of the owner's conquests above the mantle and large tusks on either side of the hearth. Family photographs and personal mementos, reflecting the owner's exciting activities, enhance this special room."

*Cordelia Cortés, Cordelia Cortés, S.A. de C.V.*
*Paseo de las Palmas 885, 3-1-1, Col. Lomas de Chapult., 11000 Mexico DF, Mexico*
*Tel.: (52) 5-202-3398, Fax: (52) 5-540-7995*

*Photography: Armando Rosales*

# Rodger Dobbel, ASID

Rodger Dobbel studied at the Chouinard Art Institute, and after a decade as a design apprentice, founded Rodger Dobbel Interiors in 1966. Mr. Dobbel is listed in the International Edition of Barons *Who's Who in Interior Design* as well as Marquis *Who's Who in the World.* A recipient of the National Philanthropy Day Distinguished Volunteer Award, he has headed many charity function to benefit such institutions as Providence Hospital, the Diabetic Youth Foundation, and Oakland's Ballet, Symphony and Museum. Mr. Dobbel has the ability to work in unlimited styles and enjoys the use of antique and contemporary accessories and furniture. His work encompasses many clients throughout the United States, as well as the greater San Francisco Bay area.

"This was an exciting, fun-filled project, as it gave me the opportunity to create and express the decorative arts in a form that I rarely have the occasion of doing. This is a second home – a country retreat, as opposed to a city-life residence of high style sleek and chic. The clay tile floors paved the way for the more casual approach to the furnishings. You will notice the wonderful antique harvest table from the region of the Pyrenees, antique French grape baskets and wood tools, combined with the salmon and blue tones of the old Persian rug and the collection of antique blue and white Chinese porcelain accessories. The framed watercolors show the talents of the owner and are different scenes of California and Arizona. The casual sophistication of the room is reaffirmed in the oil painting by the American artist, Jennefer Ross, entitled 'Summer', showing two elegantly groomed ladies leisurely boating."

*Rodger Dobbel, ASID, Rodger Dobbel Interiors*
*23 Vista Avenue, Piedmont, California 94611*
*Tel.: (510) 654-6723, Fax: (510) 658-7556*

*Photography: David Duncan Livingston*

# *Juan Jose Espiñeira*

Architect and interior designer Juan Espiñeira studied at Mexico City's La Salle University. In addition to his private practice in Mexico City, Mr. Espiñeira also serves as a consultant for the Oscar Roman Art Gallery in Mexico City, and lectures interior design at the Universidad Iberoamericana in Mexico. A member of the Mexican Chamber of Architectural Construction, his residential and contract designs have been featured in *Muebles y Decoracion* and *Entorno*.

"The gifted location of this penthouse with its splendid view of scenic Acapulco Bay dictated the concept and design of the room. Thus, I focused all of the room's decor to overlook and highlight the sea view. This concept allowed me to create a fabulous social area which consists of the dining room, bar, living room, game room and terrace. Room divisions were devised by nautical elements. A main mast with turnbuckles separates the dining area from the living room. Likewise, a stained glass wall suspended with turnbuckles, similar to those used on a ship's mast, serves as a partition between the living room and game room. Neutral colors blend smoothly with the blues and greens in the room's furnishings. Sand colored marble floor tile harmonizes with the rustic surfaces, while white walls and ceilings merge serenely with the cobalt blue of the facing walls. Large doorways provide a spectacular view of the bay from the dining room and bar area. An abundance of potted plants were placed throughout the space and on the terrace, integrating the natural forest vegetation with the entire room. The combination of design, furnishings, lighting, decoration and the natural environment creates a relaxing and leisurely space."

*Juan Jose Espiñeira*
*Anatole France No. 26, Chapultepec Polanco, Mexico D.F. 11560, Mexico*
*Tel.: (52) 5-281-4065, Fax: (52) 5-280-7259*

*Photography: Mark Boisclair*

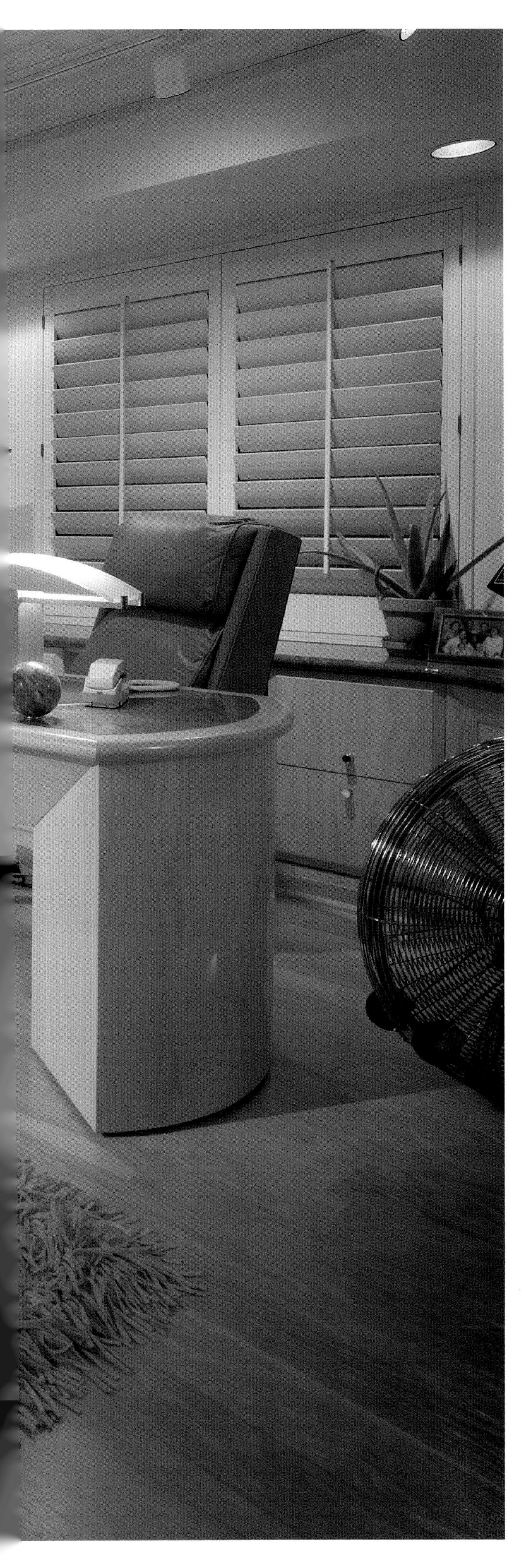

# *Kim E. Gwozdz*

Born in Spokane, Washington, Kim Gwozdz was educated at the University of Florence in Italy and received her Bachelor of Fine Arts degree from the University of Arizona. In 1988, she opened her design firm, Provenance, in Phoenix, where she serves as its principal interior designer. A member of the American Society of Interior Designers, Ms. Gwozdz has won numerous awards for her innovative projects, including the project pictured. "As each client is unique and individual, so should their interiors be," said Ms. Gwozdz regarding her design philosophy. "I do not believe in creating the same look again and again. I do believe each client deserves a space that reflects their personality and enables them to thrive in that atmosphere."

"My clients wanted a contemporary study using all of the traditional elements: wood, leather and metal. This room serves many functions, including work, relaxation, exercise, reading, enjoying the stereo or watching television. The biggest obstacle was the room's limited area. We began by agreeing that the wood should be light and the lines simple. The requirements were to have an entertainment unit which could house audio equipment and a rear projection television within a built-in unit. The floor plan limitations determined the final design scheme. Only one wall would accommodate the television, stereo equipment, books and storage. This wall, however, was interrupted by an eighteen-inch deep soffit while the television is thirty-eight inches deep. Mixing the two dimensions into a compatible solution was a challenge, solved by the use of beveled angles. The desk is the focal point of the room. Its curved sides and angled front invite approach and provide visual depth to the space. The finishes on all three custom woodwork items, desk, credenza and wall unit, are stained the same as the custom floor color. Bullnose edges in wood meet a custom *faux* granite top on the desk, while the credenza and wall unit allow the strong horizontal band of the *faux* finish to carry the eye across the spaces. Color was utilized throughout the study to visually enlarge the space. The floor and wood pieces are custom stained to match the whitewashed spruce ceiling. Walls and shutters continue the same harmonious coloration, providing an essentially monochromatic envelope. The desk chair, lounge chair and ottoman are covered in the same leather, while the *faux* granite color was developed for compatibility with this leather. The highly textured area rug provides bold relief to the many smooth surfaces and punctuates the space with an almost hidden smattering of color. The success of the room is unmistakable, while the requirements of my client were met with grace and dignity."

*Kim E. Gwozdz, Provenance, Inc.*
*2425 East Camelback Road, Suite 450, Phoenix, Arizona 85016*
*Tel.: (602) 912-8552, Fax: (602) 912-8599*

# *Anthony J. Harris*

Mexican architect Anthony Harris and his partner, interior designer Roberto Villaseca, founded Metro Cuadrado, S.A. de C.V. in 1989. With its staff of designers, engineers and decorators, the company is dedicated to the integral works in the fields of architecture, interior design, industrial design, construction and landscaping. Mr. Harris believes that three main components make his company a success: quality work completed on time at an affordable cost; design and presentations done through their 'Arris-Cad' computer software; and the company's ability to manufacture its own furniture designs. Mr. Harris has completed numerous projects in Mexico including government contracts, residential remodeling, office design and construction, such as the offices for Cabletron Systems, Inc. in Mexico City.

"The main purpose when designing this living and dining room was to make the space comfortable and warm, while integrating classic design with contemporary style. Classic design is seen in the architecture of the room, with white and gray marble floors contrasting with the contemporary glass dining table-top, and its sandblasted curved glass pedestal lighted underneath. The black lacquered chairs contrast nicely with the soft colors of the rug. Full, plush sofas, made from a white cotton, serve as the backdrop to the colorful throw pillows. The ceiling was done with gypsum in two textures mixed with various soft colored halogen lights. Personal accents in the rooms, such as the two bronze statues mounted on black marble pedestals, add elegance to the room. Transparency and privacy of space was achieved with the sandblasted glass panel."

*Anthony J. Harris, Metro Cuadrado, S.A. de C.V.*
*1A, Cda. de Gavilan No. 11, Col. San Miguel, Iztapalapa Mexico D.F., 09360, Mexico*
*Tel.: (52) 5-685-7381, Fax: (52) 5-685-5706*

*Photography: Carlos Miller*

# *Myriel Hiner*

Both an artist and an interior designer, My Hiner brings variety and drama to her design projects. Beginning her education with a B.A. in Fine Arts and continuing with extensive study in art, art history, architecture, design, ancient history and *feng shui*, she combines all with a common thread: creativity. "I approach a project as I would a blank canvas, utilizing the elements of color, line, value, texture, form, composition and balance." She owns and partners her own firms: Innova Interiors, Inc., Schmidt Boes Gallery, and My Designs; specializing in art as furniture, furniture as art. A designer of residential, commercial and art projects around the country, she has traveled extensively, been published, quoted and has lectured on design and art.

"I believe you can change people's lives through their environment. This 'California art deco' room offers an invitation to interact in a stimulating, creative experience. Black glass fireplace and large custom curved wall of wood built-ins, dominate the room. The balancing curved sectional provides an intimate setting for entertaining and conversation. I used neutrals in carpeting and textured walls as a backdrop for intense color in artwork and accessories. A juxtaposition of styles adds interest. Everything is comfortable and functional. I use art very strongly. It has a positive impact on a person's life. Bright primary colors create a happy, optimistic mood, while the sensitivity and sophistication of tribal art evokes a tranquil mood from its mysterious past. My designs are an artistic, creative medium for the awakening of a freer, more imaginative and inventive life for my clients."

*Myriel Böes Hiner, Allied Member ASID, Innova Interiors, Inc.*
*7802 Davenport Street, Omaha, Nebraska 68114*
*Tel.: (402) 392-1115, Fax: (402) 392-0188*

*Photography: Andrew Baran*

Mystical Rites and Rituals
octopus
THE SKETCHBOOKS OF PICASSO
Atlantic Monthly Press
The Pace Gallery
BALI · THE ULTIMATE ISLAND

# *Patricia Klee, ASID*

A Certified Interior Designer of commercial, residential and agribusiness complexes, as well as an architectural designer, since 1971 Patricia Klee has been the owner of her own firm, PK Design of Santa Barbara. For the past two decades she has also been a project designer, associate or design consultant for various companies and architectural firms. Her major projects include the design and development of a commercial retail center in Los Angeles, residences and ranches in the West, Southwest and Hawaii. Recently completed projects include a neo-Victorian residence in Iowa and a townhouse in Toronto, Ontario.

"The trophy room reception area and stable complex are part of a Spanish colonial ranch built to palladian scale in Santa Ynez, California. The reception area is fashioned in traditional Spanish design with its adobe textured, whitewashed stucco and modeled masonry. *Guanajuato* tiles punctuate the octagonal terra cotta pavers, while wrought iron fittings complement the beamed and paneled ceiling. Tufted leather library sofas, antique Spanish colonial tables, 19th century Vernet prints and, of course, the numerous trophies won by the stable occupants complete the interior. In the adjoining stable complex, like the trophy room, I used wood paneling, wrought iron fittings and whitewashed stucco. The high cathedral ceilings give it an airy and open quality, while sited clerestory windows provide abundant light and ventilation, housing many happy horses therein. I was privileged to be both architectural and interior designer for this project."

*Patricia Klee, ASID, PK Design*
*Post Office Box 31150, Santa Barbara, California 93130*
*Tel.: (805) 969-6102, Fax: (805) 969-0390*

*Photography: James Chen*

# *Pat Larin, ASID*

Pat Larin founded her namesake company in 1980 and has developed it into one of the leading firms in the San Francisco Bay area. A graduate of Cornell University, she is a Professional Member of the American Society of Interior Designers and is active on its Board of Directors. Her projects encompass space planning, remodeling and new construction, in addition to interior design. As a general contractor, Ms. Larin is able to provide services from conception to completion. Known for her timeless designs, she is the recipient of many awards and has been elected to *Who's Who in Interior Design*. Ms. Larin has been widely published on the local and national level, including a recent cover story in *Better Homes and Gardens*.

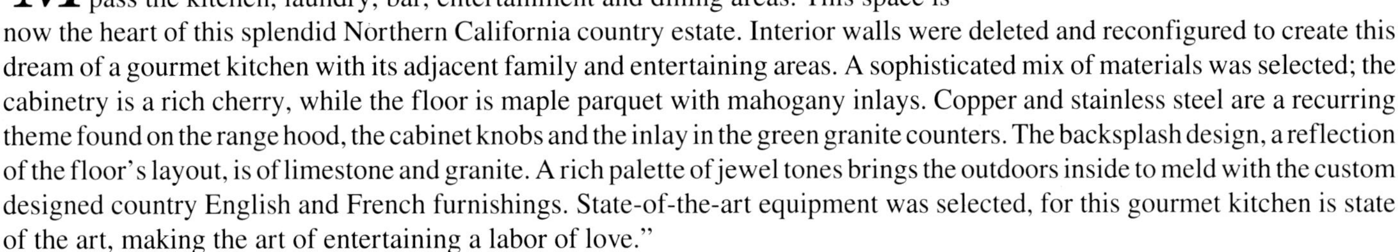
"My challenge was to create a dramatic, aesthetically pleasing space to encompass the kitchen, laundry, bar, entertainment and dining areas. This space is now the heart of this splendid Northern California country estate. Interior walls were deleted and reconfigured to create this dream of a gourmet kitchen with its adjacent family and entertaining areas. A sophisticated mix of materials was selected; the cabinetry is a rich cherry, while the floor is maple parquet with mahogany inlays. Copper and stainless steel are a recurring theme found on the range hood, the cabinet knobs and the inlay in the green granite counters. The backsplash design, a reflection of the floor's layout, is of limestone and granite. A rich palette of jewel tones brings the outdoors inside to meld with the custom designed country English and French furnishings. State-of-the-art equipment was selected, for this gourmet kitchen is state of the art, making the art of entertaining a labor of love."

---

*Pat Larin, ASID, Pat Larin Interiors*
*Certified Interior Designer #0105, Contractor's License #493031*
*12720 Dianne Drive, Los Altos Hills, California 94022*
*Tel.: (415) 941-4611, Fax: (415) 941-4047*

*Photography: John Canham*

# Cynthia Leftwich, ASID, IBD

After attending the University of Texas at Arlington, Cynthia Leftwich is currently working on a B.F.A. in sculpture at Texas Tech. Influenced to pursue a combined career by sculptor Louise Nevelson, Ms. Leftwich incorporates both art and design in each project. She has always considered her design work as art, and now realizes that her art is her design work. Her philosophy is to bring to each assignment a myriad of experience and a unique ability to communicate a client's personality through architecture, interior design and space planning. Currently, Ms. Leftwich is completing the interiors for the new Emergency & Imaging Center for the University Medical Center and the Lubbock Cotton Exchange. Although primarily a commercial designer, approximately fifteen percent of her projects are residential, including the room pictured here.

"Southwest ranch style best describes this family room located on the flat, dry, windy plains of west Texas between Mexico and Santa Fe. My client wanted to create a warm, comfortable backdrop for his collection of weavings, bronzes, traditional pottery and Navajo rugs. To achieve this western ambience, cowboy motifs, such as saddles, bridles and antique hats, were juxtaposed with the Indian artifacts to set the mood. Local artists and artisans were employed to build the furniture and paint designs of Indian hieroglyphics and hydes. Mixed with the bronzes by Glenna Goodacher and the weavings by Romeo Reyna is a cocktail table of flagstones, leather and glass, which coordinates with the floral arrangements of the patio landscape. The sculpture over the fireplace, called 'Spirits of the Wind', was commissioned by the client and executed by me as a dimensional piece, adding the feeling of song of our never-ending west Texas winds."

*Cynthia Leftwich, ASID, IBD, Shelton-Leftwich, Inc.*
*1711 Avenue J, Suite 108, Lubbock, Texas 79401*
*Tel.: (806) 747-5584, Fax: (806) 747-5586*

*Photography: Robert Suddarth*

DICTIONARY

# *Lois E. Lugonja, ASID*

Lois Lugonja majored in Fashion Design, Merchandising and Art at San Jose State University in California before launching an interior design career twenty-six years ago. In her designs, Ms. Lugonja uses her flair for dramatic color and appreciation of fabrics from her professional modeling days at the Magnin stores. Her residential projects have been published in *Better Homes and Gardens, House Beautiful, Designer West, Metropolitan Home* and *Sunset Books.* A collector of Asian art objects and antiques, her love of the Orient often appears in her accessorizing. Ms. Lugonja feels the interior must be oblivious to trends – with a careful blending of the old with the new, her designs are timeless.

"This grand house is blessed with fine architecture, including twelve-foot handcarved English wall panels, an eight-foot limestone fireplace, and a dramatic twenty-nine foot beamed ceiling. My job was to maintain the elegance of the architecture, while adding a contemporary look to the decor. To keep the charm of this large drawing room, but add a fresh look, a soft palette was selected. These shades serve as a wonderful background for the charming Lee Jofa English handprinted and coordinated fabrics. Colored in shades of rose, mauve and plum, the seating gives the room a comfortable yet elegant appearance. Classic chandeliers and the custom-designed bordered rug bring all the elements into a cohesive whole. The room is imposing, yet airy and inviting – a traditional room with refreshing, contemporary surprises."

*Lois E. Lugonja, ASID, Lois Lugonja Interior Design*
*23515 Fernhill Drive, Los Altos Hills, California 94024*
*Tel.: (415) 948-3185*

*Photography: Russell Abraham (large room photo)*

*Photography: Harold Davis*

# Gloria Roberts, ISID

Gloria Roberts was educated at Riverside Business College, the University of Southern California and Harvard School of Design. She began her career in 1958 as an assistant designer with Irving Komorrow Interiors. In 1966 she took a position as an interior designer with Binfords. Since 1979, she has been owner and principal designer of Gloria Balogh Interiors; she is married to Gaylor Wilson Singletary. In addition to being a featured speaker on radio shows and at various service clubs, Ms. Roberts has taught classes in Interior Design at Riverside Community College, Loma Linda University, and for the schools of John Robert Powers. She is also an active member of the Riverside Art Museum, the Riverside Art Alliance, and past president and charter member of the Assistance League of Riverside.

Since 1970, Ms. Roberts has been a participating designer for numerous Showcase Houses, including the Frank Miller Suite in The Mission Inn, Edgemont in 1982, Poppy Hill in 1984, and Casa Arroyo in 1986. A commercial and residential interior designer, her major projects include the conference room and president's office of Riverside Community College, and the Administration Building and University House of the University of California at Riverside, which she completed in 1990. Her work has been featured in numerous publications, including *House & Garden, House Beautiful, Better Homes & Gardens, Designers West, Interiors, Inland Empire Magazine,* and the *Los Angeles Times.*

"Elements in this guest sitting room create a tranquil old world setting of warmth and cheer. It serves as a peaceful retreat, where one can unwind and relax. From a dark panelled small room my challenge was to make it appear spacious and light. By the use of natural and intense colors and textured walls, it gave the room a tasteful elegance. The bone wallcovering provides a backdrop and the design a dynamic color. The imported Oriental design fabric in coral, blue and bone used on the daybed and the matching chair is carried to the wall and tableskirt. I selected a vibrant coral silk for the large armchair. To enhance the design I chose a mixture of French and Oriental furniture in bleached and warm rich woods. The custom designed Oriental rug features all of the colors and provides the finishing touch to this refined room."

*Gloria Roberts, ISID, Gloria Balogh Interiors*
*1733 Massachusetts Avenue, Riverside, California 92507*
*Tel.: (909) 787-9729, 724-2070, Fax: (909) 683-7291*

*Photography: Michael Irving*

# *Barbara Sande*

Commercial and residential interior designer Barbara Sande received her formal education from the University of Idaho. After obtaining her Bachelor of Arts degree, Ms. Sande worked for several design firms before establishing her own interior design company in 1987. As president, owner and principal designer of Claremont Antique and Interior, Inc., located in Claremont, California, Ms. Sande also serves as a consultant for Benefit Boutiques, Inc., a non-profit support group for hospices.

An Allied Member of the American Society of Interior Designers, Ms. Sande also holds memberships with the American Society of Appraisers, the American Society of Decorative Arts and the National Trust for Historic Preservation. Ms. Sande has been involved in several showhouses, including the Piedmont Christmas Showhouse Tour, the Piedmont Kitchen Tour, the Piedmont Benefit Guide Showhouse and the Santa Rosa Symphony Holiday Walk Benefit. Her works have been featured in *Better Homes & Gardens, Virtue Oakland Tribune* and the *Contra Costa Sun*.

"This classic country living room was designed to use the owners' collection of period antique furniture, much of the collection from their families. The antique Heriz rug is the focal point of the room, accented by the pair of Queen Anne arm chairs in blue on white wool crewel and the linen velour sofa. Textured coral is the other accent color, used in the large chair and ottoman, as well as the seats for the antique Chinese Majoan chairs.

"The crewel is used again in an antique English oak bench which sits behind the sofa. The English oak book stand and ladder-back chair are among the accessories that complement this peaceful retreat. The wood beam ceilings, stone fireplace and natural wood floors are all perfectly accented by this lovely palette of colors.

"To maximize the day's sunlight and view, I kept the window treatment to a minimum, with simple ivory draperies. For a finishing touch, I used period pieces, such as the brass containers, magazine rack and period pictures, to give this living room a comfortable and relaxed atmosphere, perfect for leisure and solace."

*Barbara Sande, Claremont Antique and Interior, Inc.*
*3529 Boyer Circle, Lafayette, California 94705*
*Tel.: (510) 299-1176*

# *Mary L. Sorenson*

Mary L. Sorenson launched Cedar Hill Design, Inc. in 1983. Using the design team approach, her firm specializes in innovative design for private residences, commercial businesses and churches. Working with her associates, licensed interior designer Cathy Rohr and account manager Gretchen Plante, Ms. Sorenson's major projects include numerous private residences, as well as Northwood University, Mountain Creek Community Church, and the Cedar Hill Chamber of Commerce.

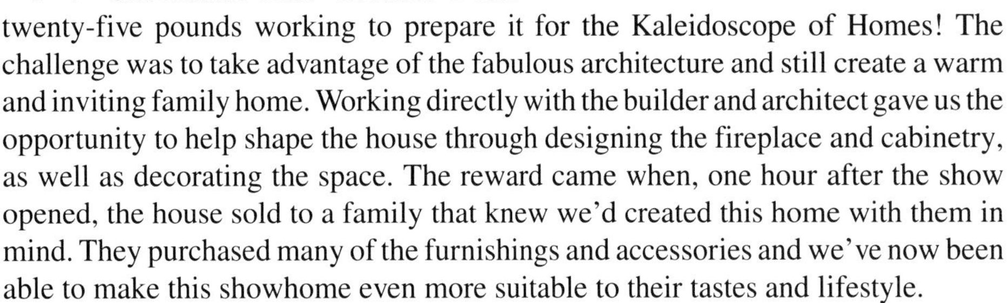

"We nicknamed this project the 'Showhome Diet' because I lost twenty-five pounds working to prepare it for the Kaleidoscope of Homes! The challenge was to take advantage of the fabulous architecture and still create a warm and inviting family home. Working directly with the builder and architect gave us the opportunity to help shape the house through designing the fireplace and cabinetry, as well as decorating the space. The reward came when, one hour after the show opened, the house sold to a family that knew we'd created this home with them in mind. They purchased many of the furnishings and accessories and we've now been able to make this showhome even more suitable to their tastes and lifestyle.

"The fireplace is hand carved of native Texas Shellstone. A floating wood floor of natural maple cued the cabinets. Insets of verde copper, stained glass cornice boards with *bouclé* yarn cascades, Corian countertops and natural materials add the ecology-minded look to match the ecology smart kitchen."

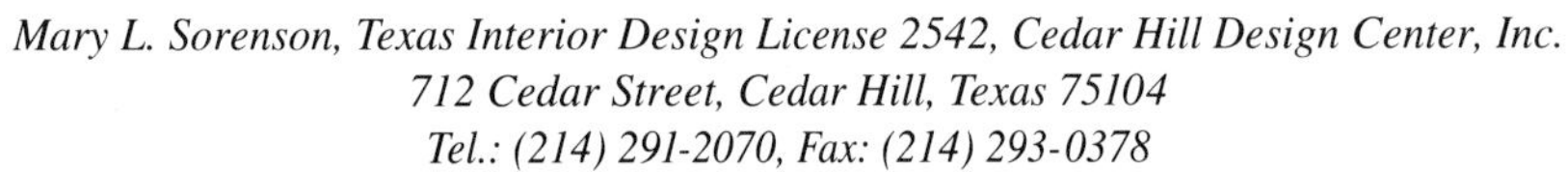

*Mary L. Sorenson, Texas Interior Design License 2542, Cedar Hill Design Center, Inc.*
*712 Cedar Street, Cedar Hill, Texas 75104*
*Tel.: (214) 291-2070, Fax: (214) 293-0378*

*Photography: Henry Biber*

# James Steinmeyer, ISID, ASID

Under his namesake firm, architectural and interior designer James Steinmeyer specializes in unique traditional, French, English, Italian and American style residences. Based in Beaumont, Texas, the firm has offices in London and Paris, designing projects in the United States, Mexico and Europe for the last thirty years. He considers the design of a house, its architecture and interiors, as a work of art. The design concepts are classic, timeless and oblivious to trends. "A James Steinmeyer design – the return to elegance."

"This bedroom, in a country chateau, was designed as a thirty-five foot square to accommodate a spectacular Qum silk rug and to afford enough space for the paintings and furnishings, while avoiding a crowded, cluttered look. The objects in this room are valued into the millions of dollars, but the criteria was to display them without creating a museum look, making the room warmly elegant and avoiding the intimidation which comes from such an important collection. It needed simplistic *Boiserie*. Louis XVI style was chosen and created in eight-inch rough cut cypress boards, then painted and glazed antique white. To enhance the effect, eleven shades of whites and glazes give the wall finish and moldings a three-hundred-year-old look. This elaborate but simple foil was necessary to complement an important collection of twelve paintings, which include a Monet, a Caravaggio, a Mauve, a pair of Sevres porcelain perfume cabinets from the boudoir of Marie Antoinette, a 17th Century head board containing a signed Canaletto oil painting, and many other splendid, signed ornate furnishings. "

*James Steinmeyer, ISID, ASID, CINOA, James Steinmeyer Associates*
*1475-85 Calder Avenue, Beaumont, Texas 77701*
*Tel.: (409) 833-7007, Fax: (409) 833-7078*

*Photography: Rob Muir*

# Edward Turrentine, ASID

Southern California designer Edward Turrentine founded Edward C. Turrentine Interior Design, Inc. in 1971. He specializes both in residential and commercial design with projects spanning the coasts from California to Maine. In 1982, Mr. Turrentine opened his current ten thousand square foot showroom, Design Center Antiques, featuring museum quality furnishings. In 1984, Design Center Fabrics was unveiled. Mr. Turrentine was awarded the IF/ASID Outstanding Residential Designer Award for both 1989 and 1991, in addition to numerous awards and commendations. His work has been featured on a number of national television shows as well as appearances in *House Beautiful, House and Garden, Los Angeles Homes,* and *Designers West*. Mr. Turrentine has been actively involved in executing various charitable events, and was a 1992 float judge for the world famous Tournament of Roses Parade.

"Venetian architectural paneling highlights this gilt living room, dictating the 18th Century European style of the space. An elegant marble fireplace serves as the focal point to this room. Framing the fireplace are very European period walls, constructed with three raised paneled areas and particular ornamentation in the proper arrangement. Old glazing, parcel gilding, tri-color silk draperies along with the newest in low-voltage lighting enhance the walls' treatment. An 18th Century rock crystal and bronze chandelier illuminates the formal center table. In line with the room's decor, I chose Scalamandre, Clarence House and Stroheim Romann fabrics to cover the museum quality court set pieces and custom upholstered furnishings. I then placed a very grandiose 18th Century Louis XVI console with its unusually thick marble top beneath the reproduction Renaissance-style painting. This fabulous console is from the famed Woolsey Estate in Pasadena, who was one of the Ziegfield girls of the 1920's. The room is reminiscent of a European mansion in its stateliness, elegance and detail."

*Edward Turrentine, ASID, Edward C. Turrentine Interior Design, Inc.*
*70 North Raymond Avenue, Pasadena, California 91103*
*Tel.: (818) 795-9964, Fax: (818) 795-0027*

*Photography: Martin Fine*

# Ron Wilson

Residential designer Ron Wilson is best known for creating the interiors for Hollywood's elite. His client list includes Johnny Carson, Cher, Michael Landon, Michael Douglas, and Kenny Rogers. As principal designer and president of his namesake Beverly Hills firm, Mr. Wilson's projects have been published in numerous international design and architecture publications, including *Architectural Digest* and *House & Garden (HG)*.

"For this grand master bedroom suite, I chose a beautiful balance between French, English and Oriental design. This house was built in a classical tradition by architect Wallace Neff, so I wanted to maintain a certain feeling of comfortable grandeur within this design.

"Two large columns serve as a natural border between the bedroom and sitting room areas. I used earth tones – cremes, grays and beiges – to create a clean and elegant appearance. The four-poster bed, three oversized lounges in creme colors sit upon two rich, thick rugs. The two large armchairs blend the soft creme color with a gentle gray. In line with the room's atmosphere, I chose light beige colored lamps. The tranquil colors of the furnishings merge nicely with the pale, natural wood floor. I used beautiful dark wood tables and stands throughout the suite to contrast the soft colors of the furnishings. Oriental vases and accent pieces, such as the traditional elephant statue and jewelry box, blend ideally with the French detailing. For a final feeling of luxury, I added numerous throw pillows to the four-poster bed, the oversized lounges and armchairs, and then accented the entire suite with an abundance of large palms."

*Ron Wilson, Ron Wilson Designer*
*1235 Tower Road, Beverly Hills, California 90210*
*Tel.: (310) 276-0666, Fax: (310) 276-7291*

*Photography: Mary E. Nichols*

# Susan Wolfe, ISID

Susan Wolfe received her B.A. in English Literature and Philosophy from the American University in Washington, DC. Having lived in Europe and the Caribbean, she settled in Mexico City in 1975, opening her store Casa Ambiente in 1976. Her projects include the Governor's residence in Toluca, Mexico, the Greek Embassy, former President López Portillo's daughter's home, the Hotel Emporio and the Mexico City homes of American automobile executives.

"Full of color, my living room combines different fabrics, styles and elements of decoration: silk *moire* on the walls, handprinted linen drapes and sofa, damask fabric on the chairs in front of the marble fireplace, a coffee table of glass and cantera stone base providing a contrast to the rich tones of wood of the furniture and bleached plank floors covered with antique Oriental carpets. The dining room has a window treatment very European in flavor combining printed linen and cotton, set off by the marble floor in colors enhancing the purity of the garden's greenness. My home provides my refuge from the hustle and bustle of the impersonal world in which we live. It has my personal stamp: it is a direct reflection of me. My 'casa' also gives me the energy and inspiration to create and be productive in my design business. This is what I give my clients: an original design using their collections and treasures in an imaginative, timeless ambiance."

---

*Susan Wolfe, ISID, Casa Ambiente S.A. de C.V.*
*Monte Athos No. 139, 11000 Mexico, D.F. Mexico*
*Tel.: (52) 5-202-0541, 5-520-8870, Fax: (52) 5-520-2050*

*Photography: Victor Benitez*

# Bettye Jordan Young

After obtaining her formal education from Georgia State University and working and living in New York twenty years, Bettye Jordan Young moved west to open her own design firm in Hollywood, B. Jordan Young, Inc. Ms. Young specializes in residential and commercial interior designs, and has completed projects throughout New York City, Southampton, Atlanta, Dallas, Palm Beach, Los Angeles and London. Her projects have been published in numerous design publications, including *Architectural Digest, Interiors Magazine, Kateigaho* and *Interior Design*.

"This living room is part of a Fifth Avenue apartment consisting of only four major rooms on the main floor of what was one of New York's finest private residences. It is used primarily for short stays in the city and business entertaining. The clients' desire was to use restraint in accommodating their needs without losing sight of the extraordinary architecture amid overblown decoration. A palette of patinated colors became the solution that calmed a fluctuating light from the west wall during the day and evened out the limited light sources in the evening. The density of colors closed down the volume to a more human scale, accomplishing the articulation of detail while necessitating less furnishings. The timeless quality achieved by this design is a subtle and traditional accent to the room's magnificent *fin de siécle* architecture."

*Bettye Jordan Young, B. Jordan Young, Inc.*
*6565 Sunset Blvd., Suite 321, Hollywood, California 90028*
*Tel.: (800) 876-0886, (213) 871-4944, Fax: (213) 876-1133*

*Photography: Derry Moore*

# *INTERNATIONAL RESIDENTIAL DESIGN*

***Jun Alday,*** South China Sea Townhouse, Hong Kong

***Samir Badro,*** Traditional Living Room, London

***Fernando Braverman,*** Entertainment Area/Living Room, Valle de Bravo

***Juckkradej Chantrakulkasem,*** Contemporary Living Room/Entry, Bangkok

***Floren de Saint Malo, ASID,*** Traditional Living Room, Panama City

***Jeanne M. Dipotontro,*** Traditional Living Room, Jakarta

***Naglaa A. Farsi,*** Salon and Veranda, Jeddah

***Mehmet Konuralp,*** Modern Living Room/Dining Room, Istanbul

***Elaine Licha, ASID,*** Contemporary Living Room/Dining Room, San Juan

***Ricardo Mayer, ASID,*** Living Room/Bar, Ipanema Beach, Rio de Janeiro

***Wajih Naccache,*** Entrance/Reception Area, Desert Palace, United Arab Emirates

***Annick Presles,*** Apartment Living Room, Caracas

***Leticia Chaves Ray,*** Country Bedroom, Asuncion

***Chiu-Hwa Wang,*** Contemporary Guest Room, Taipei

***Larry Warren,*** Luxury Villa, Sandy Lane, Barbados

***John Wilman,*** Farmhouse Lounge, Lancashire

***Flora Ye Ouyang,*** Dining Room/Karaoke Sitting Room, Sao Paulo

*Luxurious Italian benches sit beneath Mosaic art panels in the grand entrance of this oasis palace in the Al Ain desert of the United Arab Emirates. Interior design: Wajih Naccache. Photography: Dadi Motiwalla.*

# Jun Alday

Homes, hotels and corporate suites are the *forte* of Manila-born interior designer Jun Alday. With over twenty years professional experience in Hong Kong and overseas, he worked with Dale Keller & Associates, Palmer & Turner Architects, and Hirsch Bedner & Associates before setting up his own practice in 1985. Mr. Alday's works have been published in *Architectural Digest* (in the United States and Italy) and numerous regional magazines. He is also featured in the book *Contemporary Apartments* by Paige Rense. Mr. Alday's client list includes the New World Development Company, the Regent International Hotels, Shearson Lehman Brothers (Asia), Adrian Zecha, Eugene Hu and The Marquis of Headfort.

"In the Far East, one has to be sensitive to the principles of *Feng Shui* when working on design projects. I try to balance the tangible and intangible aspects of a space in order to create a positive environment that is beneficial both materially and spiritually. For this townhouse facing the South China Sea, a pair of *'fu'* lions stand guard on the roof deck to protect their owners from negative forces. The raised teak flooring provides a warm contrast to the cool ceramic tiles. Built-in amenities in an uncluttered layout allow space for *al fresco* entertaining."

*Jun Alday, Jun Alday Limited*
*19-D, Portfield Building, 10 Yuk Sau Street, Happy Valley, Hong Kong*
*Tel.: (852) 573-5529, Fax: (852) 838-2312*

*Photography: Arthur Kan*

# *Samir Badro*

A native of Aleppo, Syria, Samir Badro took his Master's Degree with honors in Architecture and Interior Design in 1970, from the Lebanese University School of Architecture and Interior Design. Fluent in Arabic, French and English, Mr. Badro spent the next several years working in Paris, Brussels and the United States. In 1975, Mr. Badro founded his own firm in Dubai U.A.E. where he has been established since. Presently, he is chairman and chief executive officer of an international network of companies located in ten cities around the world, each being fully dedicated to interior design, as well as custom furniture manufacturing. Mr. Badro's project focus, though well known for palaces and elaborate residences for foreign dignitaries, has also comprised impressive corporate headquarters, major hotels, and luxury yachts.

"Another in a series of upper scale mansions, this elegant forty-two thousand square foot residence is located in the New Market suburb of London. Horse country *par excellence*, the mood of the outdoors was captured indoors. A fine balance of colors was used to bring a homey feeling in a cold and gray environment, from the sun colors' combination of bird's-eye and birch woods, all hand-carved and hand-finished, to the matching selection of the French fabrics, and the relaxing tones of the pure wool custom-designed carpeting. With the unmatched sparkle of the Strass Italian chandeliers and its twenty-four karat gold plating, the desired ambiance was achieved. The horses were not forgotten – a hand-carved glass wall embellishes this room with an Arabian horse motif."

---

*Samir Badro, Green Line Company, Ltd.*
*Head Office: P.O. Box 5835, Sharjah, United Arab Emirates*
*Tel.: (971) 6-333-731, Fax: (971) 6-332-650*

*Branch Offices: London, Paris, Milano, Los Angeles, Miami, Singapore, Damascus, Beirut, Dubai, Abu Dhabi*

# Fernando Braverman

Born in Mexico City, Fernando Braverman first attended Universidad Iberoamericana, and then went on to receive his architecture degree from the Illinois Institute of Technology. Mr. Braverman returned to Mexico City to begin his design career in 1976. Eight years later, he founded Arquiconceptos Instalaciones, which specializes in the architecture and interior design of homes, restaurants, offices and commercial buildings.

"This room is the main entertainment area of one of nine houses located in Valle de Bravo, also known as the 'Mexican Switzerland', near Mexico City. I began by designing high beamed ceilings to give the room a feeling of spaciousness. To add drama to this area, I had a large beam mounted on the wall, accented with a row of potted vases. The dual-color treatment on the wall adds height, while integrating bright colors into the room. Inspired by Mexican tradition, the room is splashed with an abundance of bright colors. The variety of colors – turquoise, gold and beige – are used on the walls to liven the room. The turquoise color of the far wall is echoed in the floor's border tiles which blend easily with the rich, rustic Mexican tiles. The openness of the room is amplified by the profusion of natural light provided by the large view windows bordered with natural wood, overlooking the lake. To bring this outdoor ambience inside, I arranged large palm trees and other plants throughout the room. With a multitude of colors and a generous use of traditional materials, this room reflects the architectural beauty of Old Mexico in a bright contemporary setting."

*Fernando Braverman, Arquiconceptos Instalaciones, SA de CV*
*Campos Eliseos 188-402, Polanco 11560 DF, Mexico*
*Tel.: (52) 5-280-9198, 280-9573, Fax: (52) 5-281-1320*

# Juckkradej Chantrakulkasem

Born in Bangkok, Juckkradej Chantrakulkasem received his degree in interior architecture from the King Mongkut Institute of Technology. Mr. Chantrakulkasem has designed projects for the Seagate International Thailand Company, the Sriayuddhaya Bank, the Thansetthakit Newspaper Office, the Embassy of the Republic of Korea, First Pacific Asia Securities Thailand Ltd., and many private residences, hotels and offices throughout Thailand.

"Overlooking Bangkok's Chaopraya River, this spacious living room called for a contemporary interpretation of traditional style. I began by selecting simple yet rich materials, using a gray granite flooring, soft silk wall paper, mirror paneling, and a light-colored ash wood for the architectural details. For contrast, I used more colorful hues in the patterned rug design and the furniture fabrics. In the main entrance foyer I designed a unique patterned wall mirror, and specified an arched wood ceiling to create the perfect accent to the granite floor. Various traditional accent pieces complete this interior, the final design creating a mood of relaxed formality."

*Juckkradej Chantrakulkasem, The Balancing Act Co., Ltd.*
*2044/118 Chan Road, Chngnthr., Bangkok Dst./Yannawa, Thailand*
*Tel.: (66) 2-286-8795, Fax: (66) 2-392-7596*

*Photography: Voravut Suamonrattanakul*

# Floren de Saint Malo, ASID

Passionate about details, interior designer Floren de Saint Malo believes that details create the ambience of any design. Regardless of the style, whether it be eclectic, traditional or sophisticated, her philosophy is that decorative arts immediately introduce guests to that special world, her clients' habitats. Therefore, as a designer, she is always aware that a home should service its owner's way of life, introducing with her knowledge, the beauty and comfort desired. A Professional Member of the American Society of Interior Designers, Ms. de Saint Malo works in the United States and Panama.

"Since Panama is such a sunny place, personally I prefer my home to be a resting place where I can hide from the brightness. Using dark colors on the walls of my living room, immediately gets the sun out. I used purple silk *moire* and lilac colors because of my love with Claude Monet's 'Years at Giverny'. This was my inspiration for these colors. As a collector, the furniture, paintings and rugs are pieces I have acquired over the years and brought to this eclectic room that reflects my personality so well. I do believe decorating implies all the areas of a room: the floor, wall and ceiling. Although I like the eclectic look, I believe it is important to create unity and balance through symmetry and the use of colors."

*Floren Garcia de Saint Malo, ASID*
*P.O. Box 87-3195, Panama City 7, Panama*
*Tel.: (507) 64-5729, 23-5108, Fax: (507) 64-1643*

*Photography: Warren Leon, Jr.*

# *Jeanne Dipotontro, IAI*

With a background in architectural engineering and interior design, Jeanne Dipotontro has designed and developed commercial high-rise residential projects and private homes for her numerous clients. After receiving her education at the Parahyangan University in Bandung, Indonesia, Ms. Dipotontro worked as a furniture designer and architect before joining P.T. Cipta Mustika in 1976. A member of the Indonesian Architectural Association, she is currently working on the interior design and construction of exclusive apartments in Jakarta.

"My client wanted the living room of this Jakarta home to showcase her fine collection of antique ceramics, and also reflect a feeling of comfort and intimacy. To achieve this, I wanted to design a room that would be appealing to the artistic eye, and at the same time be inviting to her many guests and visitors. As a visual centerpiece, I selected a large crystal chandelier for the expansive natural wood ceiling.

"For the furnishings in this room, I specified a comfortable sofa ensemble with large plush cushions, and covered with a luxurious fabric to complement the antique sitting benches and chairs. I used this same soft colored fabric for the draperies, to offer contrast the formality of the antique furnishings. Within the large proportions of this room, one definitely senses an intimacy and comfort among the art. This living room is an ideal reflection of my client's personal style and strong artistic expression."

*Jeanne Dipotontro, IAI, P.T. Cipta Mustika*
*Jl. Let. Jend. S. Parman 78, 3rd Floor, Jakarta 11410, Indonesia*
*Tel.: (62) 21-567-1513, 567-3595, Fax: (62) 21-548-2162*

*Photography: Dr. Adrian Erwin*

# Naglaa Asaad Farsi

Naglaa Asaad Farsi studied interior design in Lebanon and is now the owner of the Silver Branch Boutique in Jeddah. Her firm is both an interior design and embroidery studio, where she specializes in restoration and the art of silver and gold embroidery. Ms. Farsi embroiders on canvas, silk, cotton, wool, satin, and various types of special materials. In the interiors field, Ms. Farsi devotes her talents to both residential projects and the design of high-end boutiques.

"High ceilings dramatized by a profusion of detailed woodwork set a striking backdrop to this Middle-Eastern salon/veranda. Dropped antique chandeliers blend beautifully with natural lighting to give the entertainment area inside this Jeddah home a comfortable yet elegant open-air environment. A hand-made wooden partition separates the veranda area from the rest of the house, making this room ideal for entertaining. The bamboo sofas, surrounded by an abundance of natural indoor plants, comfortably accommodate either small intimate conversations or large parties. The same outdoor-like theme is carried into the salon area with its marble floors, indoor plants, and ample lighting. The salon area's focal point is the beautiful Picasso masterpiece, framed by a simple bamboo sofa set and crowned with a natural rosewood ceiling."

*Naglaa Asaad Farsi, Silver Branch Boutique*
*P.O. Box 2525, Jeddah 21461, Saudi Arabia*
*Tel.: (966) 2-654-6464, Fax: (966) 2-654-9945*

*Photography: Demosthenes Perry C. Gabac, Jr.*

# Mehmet Konuralp

Lecturer and designer Mehmet Konuralp received his degree from the Architectural Association School of Architecure in London. He taught at the Architectural School in Istanbul before opening Konuralp Construction and Consulting Inc. in 1980. Mr. Konuralp's projects include numerous interiors and structures throughout the Middle East, Germany and Turkey.

"This villa on the Eastern slopes of the Bhosphorus offers a panoramic view of ancient Istanbul. I utilized the natural slope of the land to place the dining area slightly above the living room to allow maximum enjoyment of the city view. A mixture of modern Milan furnishings with traditional Turkish art creates balance. The Italian-designed glass dining set, multi-paneled wall unit and floor lamps were imported from Milan and blend elegantly with a rare 1924 Isparta-Turkey wall rug and two 1940 paintings by Turkish painter S. Akdit. The Indian quilted cover of the sofa brings subtle color to this tranquil setting."

*Mehmet Konuralp, Konuralp Construction & Consulting Inc.*
*Bostan Sokak 9/2, Tesvikiye 80200, Istanbul, Turkey*
*Tel.: (90) 212-236-1681, 212-261-2141, Fax: (90) 212-236-1680*

*Photography: Paolo Utimpergher*

50

*Photography: Joe Colón*

# Elaine Licha, ASID

A talented and innovative interior designer, Elaine Licha's projects span the United States and Puerto Rico. She received a Bachelor's degree in Art at Trinity College, and then spent a year abroad at the Institute for American University in Aix-En Provence, France. She later graduated from the Institute for Interior Design in Washington DC and pursued a degree in architecture at the Catholic University in Washington DC.

Born and raised in Puerto Rico, Ms. Licha returned to her native island after completing her education, and in 1980 opened her own design firm, Elaine Licha Interiors. As a Professional Member of the American Society of Interior Designers, Ms. Licha has held several elected positions. She was the Puerto Rico Chapter Director and Fundraising Committee Chairperson, and is served as the chapter's president during 1993. For her service, Ms. Licha was awarded the Society's distinguished Presidential Citation.

"I wanted to give this San Juan living/dining room the warmth my client desired to bring to her home. To achieve this, I chose soft pinks and bright fushias as the predominant colors throughout the room. To make the area appear spacious and casually elegant, I used minimal furnishings in each space.

"A sparkling Italian crystal chandelier shines above the unique Chinese-faced dining table. The legless table is suspended upon a black pedestal, while the custom-designed chairs are lined with a rich pink silk fabric. A large L-shaped sofa serves as the conversation area in the main seating area. Designed with a pink and fushia patterned fabric the sofa enhances the room's coziness and warmth. In line with the simple design, I placed a single glass and wood coffee table atop of the colorful rug.

"To contrast the soft colors, I used bolder colors for the living area. The flowered navy blue pattern of the love seat and lounge chair blends perfectly with the subtle creme and navy-bordered rug. I then used my client's existing collection of paintings to decorate the walls. To complete the setting, pink casement and fushia valance and moldings coordinate with the colors to give a final accent to the area's rich but relaxed appearance."

*Elaine Licha, ASID, Elaine Licha Interiors*
*Calle Taft No. 1, Apt. 15-E, Condado, San Juan, Puerto Rico 00911*
*Tel.: (809) 727-7399, 724-2070, Fax: (809) 727-7399*

# Ricardo Mayer, ASID

Born in Rio de Janeiro, Ricardo Mayer applies his knowledge of architecture and interior design to each of his commercial, retail and residential projects. Mr. Mayer studied at the Instituto La Fayette and National University before establishing his architectural firm in 1970. He is a Professional Member of the American Society of Interior Designers, as well as a member of the Cooper-Hewitt Museum in New York, and the National Trust for Historic Preservation. Mr. Mayer's architectural and interior designs have been featured in numerous publications including *Casa e Decoracao, Casa e Jardin, Casa Claudia, Arquitetura e Construcao* and *Casa Vogue*.

"This apartment is located near Ipanema Beach in Rio de Janeiro. The bar, living room and the stairway to the terrace are three distinct and well-balanced spaces forming the social area of this apartment. The soft lines of the wooden staircase are a distinguishing element in this decoration. The curved staircase, with its distinctive style and composition, leads guests to a beautiful open terrace that overlooks the stunning beaches of the city. A slightly lower-leveled floor divides the living area from the other spaces within this large room. My main concern was to disguise the hard lines of the apartment by using plaster work on the walls and ceiling. The marble floor and the pastel colored plastic paint applied to the walls as finishings appropriate to a tropical climate. Two sofas, upholstered in a light floral patterned fabric, enhance the brightness of the room. The Oriental rugs, together with master piece art works, complete the overall results with elegance and comfort."

*Ricardo Mayer, ASID, Arquitetura E Planejamento*
*680-708 Avenida Copacabana, Rio de Janeiro, Brazil 22050*
*Tel.: (55) 21-256-8616, Fax: (55) 21-256-8616*

*Photography: Juca Moraes*

# Wajih Naccache

Fluent in Arabic, French, Italian and English, Wajih Naccache is a designer on a truly international scale. He began his education at the Beaux Arts in Beirut, where he received a Bachelor's degree in Architecture. He continued his studies in Florence at the University Institute Bell Arts. Mr. Naccache relishes working on the whole project, an entire house or estate, where he can create a total environment befitting each client's personality and tastes. He has designed the interiors of numerous luxurious homes throughout the Middle East, Europe and other areas of the world.

"This grand palace is located in an oasis at Al Ain in the U.A.E. desert. With the architecture done in an Islamic style, I fashioned the entrance and reception area in a similar manner. Large double teak doors greet guests and protect the Palace from the sand. I selected Italian travertino marble for the floors, walls and skydome in the entrance. In line with the Palace's architecture, I placed Islamic Mosaic panels on the walls. The beauty of the area lies in its simplicity and radiance. The Italian Regency bench, upholstered with silk from Lorenzo Rubelli, rests between the marble pedestals and the Tabriz rug. For the adjoining reception area, The Majlis, again I specified Italian travertino marble for the walls and floors. The Musharabia is made from teak wood, the tables are made from antique brass from Marbella in Spain, and a colorful Asphahan carpet lines the floor. The area highlights the beauty of Islamic design with a touch of European grandeur and elegance."

*Wajih Naccache, Design Team*
*Naser Street, P.O. Box 1776, Sharjah, United Arab Emirates*
*Tel.: (971) 6-593-035, Fax: (971) 6-597-521, Tlx.: 68230 EM*

*Photography: Dadi Motiwalla*

# *Annick Presles*

Annick Presles apprenticed with Countess Jacqueline de Ribes in Spain and France before opening La Maison Fleurie, Inc. in Caracas in 1985. Four years later, she and partner Sophie-Eve Hocquard opened their second studio in Palm Beach, Florida. Specializing in residential, commercial and party design, their numerous projects include the decoration of the American Society Ball in honor of David Rockefeller, the celebration for Venezuelan President Carlos Andres Perez, and the American Red Cross Showcase in Palm Beach in 1990, 1991 and 1994. An antique dealer and floral designer, she has also designed the floral arrangements for numerous Saks Fifth Avenue's fashion shows.

"An architect friend gave me the fabulous idea of completely eliminating the far windows of this Caracas apartment. While this was a radical approach, the windows were not needed for structural support, and the architecture of the building is such that rain can never enter the room. The open wall gives the flat an exotic and tropical ambience, which I chose to enhance with whitewashed walls accented by dark-colored crown moldings, baseboard and door frames. Made from a tropical Venezuelan wood, these moldings give the room a warm Caribbean look. For furnishings, I first selected plush white sofas and chairs to contrast pleasantly with the dark tropical woods. A unique camel bench imported from Spain provides a humorous touch to the elegance of the space, while a strong divergence from the rustic floor is provided by the antique Persian rugs. The final blend of antiques with contemporary furnishings and accessories brings life and character to this room, creating a perfect reflection of my clients' personalities."

*Annick Presles, La Maison Fleurie, Inc.*
*The Paramount, 139 North County Road, Suite 20A, Palm Beach, Florida 33480*
*Tel.: (407) 833-1083, Fax: (407) 833-9318; Caracas, Venezuela Tel.: (582) 263-9712*

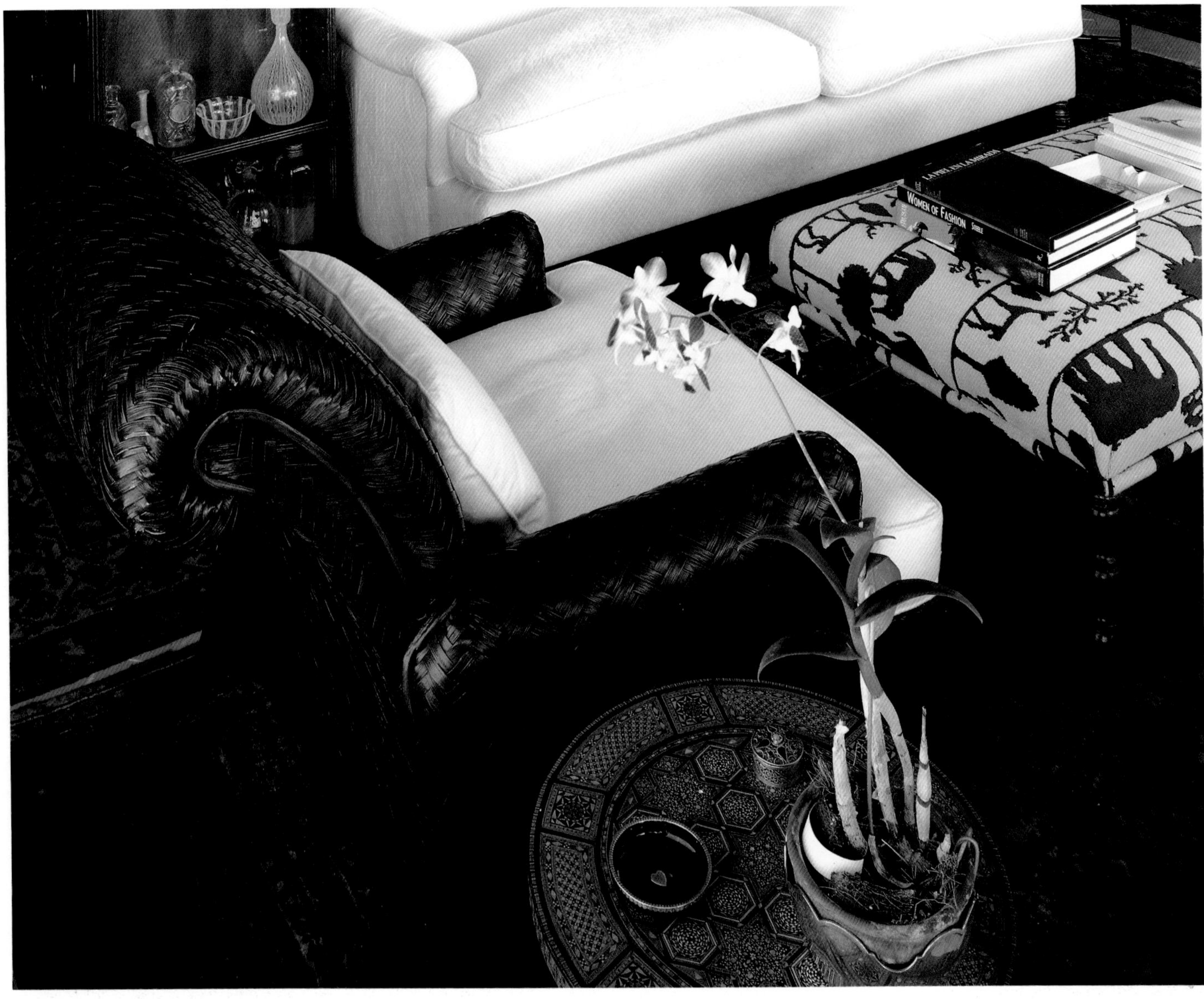


*Photography: Jose Manuel Vidaurree*

# *Leticia Chaves Ray*

Although her preference lies in residential design and restoration, Leticia Chaves Ray is equally comfortable working with commercial projects including banks, bistros, apartment buildings and corporate offices. She and her staff usually work on eight to ten major projects a year throughout her native Paraguay, and her talents have been sought out by clients in Argentina and Uruguay, as well. Ms. Ray graduated with a degree in interior design, obtained her professional interior design license, and has operated her own design studio in Asuncion, Paraguay since 1985.

"To create this romantic bedroom, I began by using a soft palette of colors. The main color scheme of pale blue and white gives this room an elegant yet cozy look. Two matching love seats surround the fireplace and glass top coffee table. A large canopy-framed bed carries the same colors and design of the love seats with a slight variation. To enhance the room's ambience, I used ceiling spotlights to give the room a warm glow. The flowered wallpaper design was also utilized on the valances to give the room a cohesive appearance. Finally, a hope chest and coordinated accent pieces were added to complete this comfortable and charming space."

*Leticia Chaves Ray*
*Mariscal Estigarribia 1636, Asuncion, Paraguay*
*Tel.: (595) 21-200-612, Fax: (595) 21-210-846*

# Chiu-Hwa Wang

After receiving her B.A. in Architecture from the National Central University in Chungking, China, Chiu-Hwa Wang traveled abroad to complete her formal education. She studied at the University of Washington and obtained her Master's in Architecture from Columbia University. A noted architect, Ms. Wang has taught her craft at several universities in the United States and Taiwan. With her practice based in Taipei, Ms. Wang has won several honors for her various projects, including the Taiwan Provincial Building Design Award and the Gold Plaque Award from the Chinese Architect Annual.

"This penthouse on the seventh floor roof of my own residence apartment is used as a guest suite, for tea parties and, occasionally, for teaching a seminar class. The built-in desk, bookcase and wardrobe wall allow for maximum use of space. The *tatami* floor without furniture provides a sleeping area for four or a seating area for up to twenty people. The room is furnished in wood, except for one white plastered wall, which serves as a projection screen for slides or movies. The roof slopes from north to south, providing for a solar collector on top and clerestory windows for cross ventilation. The 'floral' window, an old Chinese motif, opens to the garden terrace."

*Chiu-Hwa Wang, Architect*
*21, Alley 12, Lane 118, Ren Ai Road, Section 3, Taipei, Taiwan*
*Tel.: (886) 2-701-2617, Fax: (886) 2-700-4489*

*Photography: John Ngai*

# Larry Warren

Born and raised in Barbados, Larry Warren obtained a degree in Environmental Studies from the University of Manitoba in Canada in 1978. Three years later, Mr. Warren received his Master's Degree in Architecture from the same institution. Upon completion of his studies, he returned to Barbados, working for Robertson Ward Associates. In 1986, Mr. Warren opened his own design and architectural firm and has since served as its sole principal.

"What I enjoyed most about designing this luxury villa on the exclusive Sandy Lane in Barbados was the opportunity to work on the whole project, from conception to completion. For the outside architecture of the villa, I chose a Barbadian design. Built of timber fenestration and verandas, the design of the villa enhances the tropical environment of the Island. For the interior, I wanted to incorporate the tropical theme of the exterior and bring it indoors. I chose a classic design to complement the grand style of the living room with its large columned arches. I surrounded the coral stone top coffee table with three sofas and a large sectional. The vibrant violet color of the table is enhanced by color of the seating, upholstered of a light green and violet fabric. Four matching table lamps of lilac also amplify the rich colors of the room. The symmetry of the arches, chandeliers and coral stone provides a timeless and elegant island ambience."

*Larry Warren, Larry Warren Architect Ltd.*
*Derricks, St. James, Barbados*
*Tel.: (809) 432-6392, Fax: (809) 432-2976*

*Photography: Robbie Davis*

# John Wilman

Born in Lancashire, England, John Wilman studied textile design at the Manchester Regional College of Art. He has won numerous awards for his adaptations of Parisian designs for the contemporary British market. Joining the Reed Paper Group in 1967, he worked in the Crown Studio for ten years before moving to Coloroll's Wallcoverings. Mr. Wilman headed up the design team that launched Coloroll into the home fashion market under its own name, and has become the second largest wallcovering company in the country. John Wilman's Shalimar concept of lighting, ceramics, carpets, beds, and upholstered furniture, designed in 1987, rapidly became one of Coloroll's most successful collections.

In 1990, with partner Eric Kilby, he founded his own company, which currently offers six designer collections under the John Wilman Fabrics and Wallpapers brand name. Along with his fabric designs, Mr. Wilman has worked on numerous residential and contract interior design projects throughout the United States, England, France and Europe.

"The lounge of my farmhouse in Lancashire has the unique charm that one can find only in a genuine period building. Upon entering this room, one's attention is immediately drawn to the large stone fireplace. The raised hearth is recessed deeply into the wall, the back of which features a quaint and rustic patina that is the result of fires burning against it for many, many years. While now seldom used for open fires, this fireplace still brings warmth to the room through the antique stove placed within its walls. A strong and purposeful architectural statement is also made by the three massive oaken ceiling beams, each nearly a foot thick and nearly as wide. These solid and rough-hewn beams act as a strong visual element, their direction again reinforcing the imposing quality of the stone hearth. Both the massive fireplace hearth and these large oak ceiling beams are architectural qualities which practically demand that a classical design be maintained throughout this room. To accent these features, I selected a rich gold and turquoise fabric for the draperies, and luxurious silk for the chairs and matching throw pillows. The walls are painted a soft white, serving as a backdrop to the many paintings, some modern, some traditional. To again accent this room's strong architecture, I specified a soft gray carpeting. Throughout the design, a combination of textures and colors, along with a careful mixture of old and new, brings a feeling of warmth, making this room the restful and inviting chamber I wanted to create."

*John Wilman, John Wilman Limited*
*Riverside Mills, Crawford Street, Nelson Lancashire, England BB9 7QT*
*Tel.: (44) 282-617-777, Fax: (44) 282-614-222*

*Photography: Mark Wilman*

# Flora Ye Ouyang

After teaching architecture and interior decoration at several colleges in Taiwan, Flora Ye Ouyang worked in the construction department of Chaing Kai Sheck International Airport. She was responsible for both the landscaping design, and airport hotel, flight kitchen and terminal interior design. Ms. Ye Ouyang moved to Brazil in 1975 and continued her education at FAU Universidade de Sao Paulo. Today, in addition to her architectural firm, Ms. Ye Ouyang also owns two factories, one producing custom glasswork, and the other specializing in fabric upholstery. The trio of companies work together closely to support and implement her creative ideas.

"This dining room/karaoke sitting room was designed for evenings of food, friends and entertainment. Beginning with the dining area, I selected a large round glass-top dining table, which can comfortably seat up to fourteen guests. Accented with custom-designed skirted chairs, the table features a smaller rotating glass disk that allows for easy food service. After a festive meal, guests can retreat to the karaoke area, where five sofas, placed in a U-shaped fashion, offer an abundance of comfortable seating. On the center of the beautiful stand is the wide karaoke picture screen and on both sides are collections of Brazilian semi-precious stone sculptures placed upon the thick crystal shelves and spotlighted from above with focused light. Adjoining this area is a mini-golf course, complete with a motor-controlled glass roof and walls, which converts the space into a mirror-walled gymnasium."

*Flora Ye Ouyang, Yei Projeto e Objeto Ltda. and Yei-House Ltda.*
*Rua Manoel Mendes Fernandes 29, Jd. Paulista, Sao Paulo, Brazil, 04507-030*
*Tel.: (55) 11-887-7490, 11-887-9350, Fax: (55) 11-884-7873*

*Photography: Fifi Tong*

POP....
ROCK AND
SOUL
THE CHART
FROM THE U.K
M AND U.S.A.
JUNIOR JOE
BY JOE BLOGGS
BIG STAR
VARSITY
ROMANCE

# *WORLDWIDE CONTRACT DESIGN*

***Olivier-Clement Cacoub,*** Grand Salon of Honor, Tunis

***Moon-Young Choi,*** Formal Restaurant, Paradise Hotel, Cheju Island, Korea

***Henry Conversano,*** Bistro Restaurant, Mirage Hotel, Las Vegas

***Antonio de Garay,*** AT&T Headquarters, Mexico City

***Bernardo de Silva,*** Executive Office, Monterrey

***Melanie Doss, ASID,*** Attorney's Office, Nashville

***Foo Fatt Chuen,*** Executive Office Suites, Kuala Lumpur

***Marisabel Gómez Vázquez de Morales,*** Ritz-Carlton Hotel, Cancun

***Bosco Gutierrez Cortina,*** Santa Maria Ranch, Aguascalientes, Mexico

***Bosco Ho,*** Main Reception Area, Beijing Qian Men Hotel, China

***Masae Kawamura, JID, JIA,*** Lobby Lounge, Pacific Hotel Chiba, Japan

***Nancy Kwok, MCSD,*** Hawaiian Restaurant, Beijing Gloria Plaza Hotel, China

***Wilfried Lachermair,*** Rolf Tillmanns Men's Fashion Store, Germany

***Juan Domingo Leaño,*** Hotel Suites, El Mesón Doña Paz Resort, Mexico

***Sarah Tomerlin Lee,*** Bellevue Hotel, Philadelphia

***Heinz-Werner Maden, BDIA,*** Vital Hotel Royal, Tyrol, Austria

***Midori Manabe, ASID,*** The Park Suite, Imperial Hotel, Tokyo

***Yorgos Maryelis,*** Mediterranean Travel Station, Greece

***Ahmed Nour,*** Pool and Health Club, Kuwait Meridien Hotel, Kuwait City

***Eui-Jo Oh,*** Trad Club Men's Store, Seoul

***Joshua J. Pan, FAIA,*** TASA Construction Company Corporate Offices, Taipei

***Ed Poole, AIA, RAIA, SIA,*** Royal Sporting House, Singapore

***Carlos A. Profet,*** Seaport Casino, Oranjestad, Aruba

***Chavivan Rujimora,*** Executive Dining Room/Lounge, Bangkok

***Yozo Shibata, JIA,*** Atrium, Haneda Air Terminal, Japan

***Vipwal Singhakowin,*** Chalermkrung Royal Theatre, Bangkok

***John Wendover,*** Medical Office, Montreal

***Gaby Widajanti, HDII, IAI,*** Reception/Lounge Area, Modern Bank, Jakarta

***Evan Williams,*** Main Pavilion, Sandals La Toc Resort, St. Lucia, West Indies

***Jaci Yoap, IFDA,*** Hunt Library Showroom, Lake Michigan

***Hugh Zimmern,*** Michelle's Restaurant, Hong Kong

---

*An air of mystery is designed into this unusual retail showroom, with the display chambers floating on hidden supports, one material never touching the next. Interior design: Ed Poole, AIA, RAIA, SIA. Photography: Seow Cheong Heng.*

# Olivier-Clement Cacoub

A recipient of the coveted Premier Grand Prix de Rome, Olivier-Clement Cacoub studied architecture at Ecole des Beaux Arts, and is currently the principal of his architectural firm in Paris. All his projects offer a diverse abundance of grandeur with aesthetic harmony. Mr. Cacoub has done major projects in Paris (le Ponant), Nanterre (Dumez), Tunis, the Ivory Coast, Zaire, Senegal, Cameroon, the former Soviet Union, Morocco, Tahiti, New Guinea, Jordan, Portugal, and various other locations throughout the world.

"Upon entering the galleries of this Grand Salon of Honor in Tunis, one's attention is immediately taken by the three great chandeliers. Each is six meters wide, eight meters high, and contains ten thousand pieces of crystal, all suspended from three grand domes. In the evening, these majestic pieces illuminate the ballroom, enhancing the rich materials used throughout the salon. The large Venician stained glass windows are accented by the fifteen hundred meters of Italian marble – laid in a parquetry design – which is used for the flooring and columns. The furniture is a mixture of Tunisian and Louis XVI-style, as seen in the console, cabinet, buffet table and bases, while rich Persian and Tunisian silk rugs line the floors. Used for official receptions, state dinners and award ceremonies, this Grand Salon is the successful merger of two cultures: the architecture of European formality with the lavishness of Middle Eastern decoration."

*Olivier-Clement Cacoub, Architecte en Chef des Batiments Civils et Palais Nationaux*
*54, avenue d'Iena, 75116 Paris, France* — *88, avenue d'Iena, 75116 Paris, France*
*Tel.: (33) 1-47-20-08-23, Fax: (33) 1-47-20-42-58* — *Tel.: (33) 1-47-20-35-49, Fax: (33) 1-47-23-65-81*

# Moon-Young Choi

Korean designer Moon-Young Choi specializes in commercial and residential interior architecture and design. He received his Bachelor of Fine Arts degree from Hong-Ik University in Seoul, and his Interior Design diploma from Rhodec Design School in England. Mr. Choi has been working as a professional designer for over thirty-five years in Korea and overseas. His recent projects include the Paradise Hotel in Sogwipo, Che-Ju Island, several Polo/Ralph Lauren Stores in Korea, and the entire design concepts of numerous Citibank retail branches throughout Korea.

"The Paradise Hotel on Korea's Che-Ju Island is one of the finest resort hotels in the far eastern region, with its unique facilities surrounded by beautiful ocean and mountain vistas. Within this beautiful natural environment, I adapted the design concept with an old Mediterranean style. The restaurant featured here is the main area of activity, where hotel guests enjoy their meals and services. The rustically treated rough, naturally finished wooden ceiling beams were designed to match the plastered walls and archways. The furnishings were custom designed in the primitive motif of the Middle Ages to give this interior a dreamy and relaxed feeling of fantasy."

*Moon-Young Choi, M.Y. Design Office*
*Han-Nam Dong 707-34, Yong-San Ku, Seoul, Korea*
*Tel.: (82) 2-749-2077, Fax: (82) 2-749-2075*

*Photography: Ok-Rei Cho*

# *Henry M. Conversano*

In his thirty years as a hotel and restaurant interior designer, Henry Conversano has won numerous accolades for his grand and diverse projects. A recipient of the Nevada Contractor's Silver State Award for his design of the Mirage Hotel & Casino in Las Vegas, he also received the 5 Diamond Award for the design of Harrah's Hotel & Casino in Lake Tahoe. Since the 1961 opening of his design company, Conversano & Associates, Mr. Conversano's work has showcased the most innovative and splendid works in the hospitality field. A partial list of his projects include the new Las Vegas MGM Grand Hotel & Casino, the Las Vegas Hilton, the Showboat Hotel & Casino and Bally's Grand Hotel & Casino in Atlantic City, The Lost City in Sun City, South Africa, and the Reno Hilton in Nevada.

"A grand columned archway entices diners into the beautiful Bistro Restaurant, one of four restaurants I designed in the Mirage Hotel. As a grand entrance, four colorfully decorated columns support the dome-shaped archway leading to the brass entry doors. Each column has its bright turquoise backdrop adorned with vibrantly colored flowers. Numerous colorful potted flowers are arranged along the walkway and archway, leading to an entrance which is equally ornate. Once inside the restaurant, one is transported to the Paris of the 1920's. Styled in a uniquely Parisian *art nouveau* brasserie fashion, the entire design of The Bistro is true to the era it recaptures. A bronze statue sits beneath the majestic stained glass ceiling dome. Rich mahogany is used throughout the ceiling and paneling, while bold black-and-white marble tile lines the floor. I chose to contrast the weight of the architecture with softer, more subdued furnishings, using period-style rattan chairs and tables draped with pale peach tablecloths."

*Henry M. Conversano, Conversano & Associates*
*5758 Broadway, Oakland, California 94618*
*Tel.: (510) 547-6890, Fax: (510) 547-3807*

BISTRO
VIA
ELENA

# Antonio de Garay A.

Born in 1948, Antonio de Garay obtained his degree in Architecture from the National University of Mexico. In 1976, he founded his own firm in Mexico City. Mr. de Garay has been head of construction work for some of the leading public and private institutions in Mexico, and has been selected to participate in bidding on architectural projects throughout the country. His firm specializes in the design of office buildings and interiors.

"For the AT&T Headquarters in Mexico City, I began by creating an individual image that reflects the smart and efficient operation desired by my clients. However, aesthetics and beauty were the driving forces of this architectural design. In my architectonical work, I have approached contemporary Mexican architecture as though it were a landscape that lives from the morning light to the mystery of the shadows, all this supported by colors and textures that remain the presence of the earth, the sun, the water and the wind."

*Antonio de Garay, Antonio de Garay Arquitectos Asociados*
*Petrarca 223-204, Col. Polanco, Mexico D.F. 11560, Mexico*
*Tel.: (52) 5-250-5241, Fax: (52) 5-203-1368*

*Photography: Alberto Moreno Guzman*

# Bernardo De Silva

Born and raised in Monterrey, Mexico, Bernardo De Silva is on the cutting edge of interior design. Taking the all-around approach in his works, he is involved in each aspect of his projects, from planning and design and on through to fabrication and final installation. As acting president of the eight-hundred-person Vexon Group, his company has taken an assertive market- and growth-oriented stance in the design field.

"Only a few years ago, our competitors were nationally-based companies. We managed to out-perform firms which at the time were industry leaders," Mr. De Silva said of the company's rapid and successful rise. "What really inspires our group is our ability to compete at the world's highest levels. Our challenge is to continually expand Vexon's client base throughout the international marketplace."

In the past year, Mr. De Silva completed the design for Balsa Industries, and also supervised the complete renovation of Vexon's offices. In his own office, we can see the 'vanguard' style he brings to his designs.

"The designing of my private office at The Vexon Group presented the perfect opportunity to exhibit my work to potential clients. When clients enter this office, I want them to see an efficient, professional and comfortable space."

"To achieve this, I chose to mix modern design and traditional Mexican flavor. My desk is a prototype of a modern design with its simple lines, lacquered black top and glass legs. Similarly, the leather chairs are fashioned in the same mode. To contrast the modern look against the elements of Mexican style, I placed a quarry stone wall next to the desk and spotlighted the numerous Mexican paintings on the walls.

"I carried the modern theme from the contemporary furnishings and integrated it throughout the room. Within the wall, an exquisite crystal sculpture is displayed. Other glass and crystal accent pieces rest upon the large glass coffee table and still others are placed throughout the office. Mexican style is also an integral component of the design, seen in the rich, colorful rug and matching wall treatment. To complete the setting, a plush sofa and armchair create an area for both relaxed conversation and serious business discussions. This office, surrounded by a peaceful atmosphere, invites one to work with precision and efficiency."

*Bernardo De Silva, The Vexon Group, S.A.*
*Gonzalitos No. 456 Sur, Monterrey, Nuevo Leon 64050, Mexico*
*Tel.: (52) 8-333-5133, Fax: (52) 8-333-2288*

*Photography: Eduardo Gonzalez*

# *Melanie Doss, ASID*

After working with several top architectural firms, Melanie Doss returned to her alma mater, the University of Tennessee, as an instructor, and recently opened Doss Design Associates in Knoxville. A Professional Member of the American Society of Interior Designers, she served as the Tenessee Chapter's president. Along with projects for Kimberly-Clark Corp., Ms. Doss has designed several projects for the University of Tennessee, including the John C. Hodges Library, the Gibbs Hall Athletic Facility and its football facility.

"The image desired by my client was that of a solid and successful attorney with traditional values, conducting business in a professional and progressive manner. The challenge was to incorporate the following criteria within a space of approximately five hundred twenty square feet, while accentuating the breathtaking view of downtown Nashville from the twenty-eighth floor office of the Stouffer Tower. Within this office, I needed to provide ample room for the principal attorney's work area, his paralegal, client files, reference materials, a client interview area and private bath and dressing area. The solution was the creation of a comfortable and efficient yet exciting office maximizing the vertical space, using light but rich finishes, and featuring the client's original art and sculpture collection. For the attorney's work area, two small pendant fixtures suspend above the desk emphasizing the custom furniture system. Two teal and gold patterned loveseats and a classic *noguchi* table function as the interview area. The paralegal's work space is located beyond the entry for visual and acoustical privacy.Wood, maple stained to a silkened finish, is the primary design element with color and texture expressed in the accent pieces, sculptures and paintings. The minimal window treatment simply affords ultimate viewing of the cityscape. The resulting solution was the creation of a comfortable and efficient yet exciting office environment using light but rich finishes and properly expressing the client's work ethic and style."

*Melanie Doss, ASID, Doss Design Associates*
*602 South Gay Street, Suite 102, Knoxville, Tennessee 37902*
*Tel.: (615) 637-4149, Fax: (615) 523-7949*

*Photography: Bill LaFevor (room), David Luttrell (portrait)*

# *Foo Fatt Chuen*

The recipient of the 1990 Worldstone's International Award, Foo Fatt Chuen has showcased his work in commercial, residential, retail and hotel designs throughout Europe and Asia. Mr. Foo is the principal designer for Axis Network in Kuala Lumpur, and a Professional Member of the Malaysian Institute of Interior Designers. He received his architectural diploma from Polytechnic University of Central London, and began his design career in London before moving to Malaysia.

"As the majority of our projects are hotels, we decided that our own offices should be more experimental, using materials which we do not normally use. The various public areas of the office are a juxtaposition of simple materials. I used untreated mild steel on the walls and ceilings, vinyl floor tiles on walls and tabletops, and stainless steel on the door fins. Lighting is treated as atmospheric in the public areas, using low voltage and metal halide. The overall design gives a striking perspective to all who enter."

---

*Foo Fatt Chuen, Axis Network*
*Suite 7.15, 7/F, Wisma Central, Jalan Ampang, 50450, Kuala Lumpur, Malaysia*
*Tel.: (60) 3-263-4181, Fax: (60) 3-263-4186*

*Photography: Picture This & That*

# Marisabel Gómez Vázquez

Marisabel Gómez Vázquez takes pride in having successfully designed projects for major hotel operators and developers. She has designed spaces for the Ritz-Carlton, Marriott, Hyatt, Sheraton, Nikko, Melia and Fiesta Americana chains throughout Mexico and Latin America. She obtained her degree in Interior Architecture and Design, with studies in México, Europe and the United States. Ms. Gómez is the director and vice president of Arquitectura de Interiores with a staff of thirty professionals. Her firm, strongly established in México as one of Latin America's leading interior design companies, is part of a corporate group of architects, interior designers, landscape designers and urban planners. Ms. Gómez's works have been published in *Restaurant and Hotel Design International, Casas y Gente, Resorts and Great Hotels* and *Auge de México.*

"Simple elegance is the distinctive touch of the Ritz-Carlton Cancun Hotel. Our goal in designing this hotel was to enhance the Mexican cultural heritage combined with classic European style. The exquisite *art nouveau* style brought to Yucatán by the French was my inspiration in designing this restaurant. The architectural details, such as the hand-carved wood moldings and softly lit cove ceilings, blend together with rich textures and furnishings. Hand-wrought iron chandeliers patinaed in terra cotta are set against the soft peach colors of the walls and draperies. The dining chairs, which reflect the carving design of the window moldings, combine the peach tones with a light green and accentuate the colors of the carpet. Dining tables nestle around a grand piano with spectacular views of the Caribbean. To contrast the softness of the decor, rich wood furnishings were used. The lobby is appointed with fine hand-carved antiques, lavishly upholstered sofas and chairs and custom designed wool area rugs, creating an atmosphere of classic elegance and intimate sophistication."

*Marisabel G.V. de Morales, Arquitectura de Interiores*
*Aurelio Ortega 764 Col. Seattle, Guadalajara, Mexico 45150*
*Tel.: (52) 3-656-2939, Fax: (52) 3-656-5747*

*Photography: Scott McDonald of Hedrich-Blessing*

# Bosco Gutierrez Cortina

After graduating from the Universidad Iberoamerica, Bosco Gutierrez worked at Legorreta Architects in Mexico City before opening his namesake firm in 1983. His projects have been featured in a number of professional publications, including *L.A. Architect, Architectural Record, Designers West, Mexico Nueva Arquitectura, Casas y Gente* and *Artes de Mexico*. Mr. Gutierrez believes that rather than being separate entities, architecture and interior design come together as integral components of every project.

"This public area of the Santa Maria Ranch in Aguascalientes, Mexico, presented the challenge of creating a warm atmosphere within a small, confined space. The room itself is bordered by two patios, and we wanted to integrate the three areas into one. To increase the overall spaciousness of the room, we first specified an eighteen-foot wooden beam ceiling, and then called for large windows and a glass multi-paneled arched door to lead into the adjoining hallway. In harmony with this room's traditional Mexican architecture, we used natural, aged materials, placing an emphasis on texture and color. As a final accent, we selected a rich, warm color for the walls to complement and blend with the natural materials used throughout the space, thereby giving this room its serene and peaceful feeling."

*Bosco Gutierrez, Gutierrez Cortina Arquitectos S.C.*
*Emilio Guerrero/Fernando Cardenas/Alejandro Medina Asc. Architects*
*Av. Revolucion, No. 1373, Col. Campestre, 01040 Mexico D.F., Mexico*
*Tel.: (52) 5-662-0190, Fax: (52) 5-662-9816*

*Photography: Alberto Moreno Guzman*

# *Bosco Ho*

Architect and interior designer Bosco Ho is a graduate of Hong Kong University. A member of the Royal Institute of British Architects, he has implemented and designed numerous offices, shopping centers and residences throughout Asia. A few of his major projects include the headquarters of the Kader Industrial Company, the Chingtechen Hotel, the Hong Kong Housing Society Hung Hom redevelopment, the New Airport Railway Kowloon Station in Hong Kong and the Carrianna Friendship Square at Shenzhen, China.

"The design of the Beijing Qian Men Hotel's main reception area represents the fusion of traditional Chinese style with modern elegance. At the far end of the space, a round-shaped atrium is enshrouded in natural light coming through the skylight. Sunlight supplied by the skylight not only enhances the beauty of the surroundings, but also brings out the theme of the decorative work. The floor of the main lobby is tiled with granite and the pillars are mounted with white, jade-like slate. Materials used in the reception and check-out counters are decorated in gold, suggesting warmth and elegance. During the winter, the adjoining courtyard supplies the atrium with warmth and brightness. The surroundings of the atrium are decorated with a simple and natural brick, while in the middle of the yard is a unique fountain which represents the Chinese symbol of inexhaustible wealth."

*Bosco Ho*
*B63, Provident Centre, Wharf Road, North Point, Hong Kong*
*Tel.: (852) 811-5733 x. 670, Fax: (852) 5-811-5775, 5-811-5904*

# Masae Kawamura, JID, JIA

Multi-faceted interior design projects are standard for Masae Kawamura, Executive Director of Kanko Kikaku Sekkeisha, Yozo Shibata & Associates, the prestigious Tokyo-based design firm. The firm is considered a leading hotel planning design office, with a history spanning thirty-two years in Japan and abroad. Often encompassing a wide range of space and facility needs, a single project may include restaurants, lounges, meeting rooms, ballrooms, retail shops, pool areas, gymnasiums and other recreational facilities. The fabulous project featured here was designed by Masae Kawamura and the firm's president, Yozo Shibata. Mr. Shibata and Mr. Kawamura hold a philosophy that architect and interior designer should create according to the needs of society and the desires of the community.

"A magnificent six-tiered crystal chandelier is the crowning jewel to the stunning lobby lounge of the Pacific Hotel Chiba, located in one of Tokyo's largest satellite cities. As one's first impression of the hotel, I strove to represent the interior character of the hotel with a combination of stylish furniture, modern details in the architectural elements, and contemporary art work. To make the room inviting, I chose to design it in warm tones with the cherry plywood and soft colors of the furnishings. The clear Indian sandstone, dark Italian marble, crystals and polished bronzes provide a sharp contrast to the light tones. The final result is exactly what our client desired: an entrance that is at once striking, dramatic and luxurious."

*Masae Kawamura, JID, JIA, Kanko Kikaku Sekkeisha, Yozo Shibata & Associates*
*No. 17 Mori-Building, Toranomon 1-26-5, Minato-Ku, Tokyo 105, Japan*
*Tel.: (81) 3-3507-0376, Fax: (81) 3-3507-0386*

# *Nancy Kwok, MCSD*

Since the start of her career in 1972, Nancy Kwok has developed exceptional expertise in all areas of interior design. Her projects include commercial designs, hotels, offices, shopping malls and restaurants. After having worked for several prominent design firms, she started operating her own firm, Hinex Universal Design Contracting Co. Ltd., in 1986. Among Ms. Kwok's numerous recent projcets are the Bank of China's Headquarters Building in Shenzhen, China, the headquarters for the Xin Hua News Agency (NCNA) in Macau, the Beijing Gloria Plaza Hotel in China and the seven-story Oriental Rainbow Department Store in Shenzhen.

"This Hawaiian restaurant is located in China's Beijing Gloria Plaza Hotel. My first goal with this design was to create an inviting tropical feeling within this very spacious room. I began by visually separating the room into sections. I designed a circular space with a domed ceiling to act as a partition between the dining area and the buffet tables. This gives the room unity, while gently regulating its space. Columns of varying sizes were then placed throughout the room to create an illusion of intimacy. The elegant buffet table was designed for convenient access on both sides, to allow for easy traffic flow. In keeping with the island theme, I placed traditional Hawaiian wooden sculpture and various decorations and accent pieces throughout the restaurant. The completed design gives diners an experience of the tropics within the comfort of this magnificent hotel."

*Nancy Kwok, MCSD, Hinex Universal Design Contracting Co., Ltd.*
*Rm. 3102, Top Glory Tower, 262 Gloucester Road, Causeway Bay, Hong Kong*
*Tel.: (852) 833-0228, Fax: (852) 833-0223*

*Photography: Daniel Design and Production*

# *Wilfried Lachermair*

In 1976, Wilfried Lachermair started his own architectural firm, Planen und Bauen GmbH, specializing in retail construction. He expanded the firm in the mid-1980's, adding a business-sector branch with emphasis on independent shop concepts for renowned stores. Mr. Lachermair's latest addition to his firm is a consulting arm that provides counsel in the areas of merchandising, space organization and retail design. With these three divisions, the Lachermair group covers all areas involved with retail problem solving.

"My client, Rolf Tillmanns, wanted to create an optical impression of transparency and space in his men's fashion store in Rhineland, Germany. To give the illusion of openness, I began by having the former courtyard area covered with a glass daylight dome. I then designed the walls and dropped ceiling to form a visual frame around the room. For color, I repeated the light tones of the speckled granite floor tiles in the white lacquered walls. To make the room appear larger, I contrasted round shapes – in the pillar designs and footings of display tables – with the sharp right angles of the wall shelves. The overall design of this space relies upon light, architectural accents, and contrast in shape and materials used throughout the store."

*Wilfried Lachermair, Planen und Bauen GmbH*
*Talstr. 25, 42697 Solingen, Germany*
*Tel.: (49) 212-79055, Fax: (49) 212-79050*

*Photography: Rainer Eickmeyer*

# Juan Domingo Leaño

Architect Juan Domingo Leaño Reyes is the Director General of Isla Navidad, a resort that is being developed by Turbana, S.A. de C.V., in Manzanillo, Mexico. El Mesón Doña Paz, the welcoming center of Isla Navidad, the tourist, golf and nautical resort, opens its doors, rooms, balconies and corridors to the Mexican Pacific Ocean and the Barra de Navidad Lagoon.

"With an architectural design of ample and bright spaces, the comfortable suites at El Mesón Doña Paz blend the elements of the Mexican landscape to create a cozy and festive atmosphere. I chose to contrast the rich colors of the ceramics, textiles, glazed tiles, copper, and wooden beams against the brightness of the white walls and plush seating. Ample seating in the lobby is provided by the neutral-colored sofa and armchairs. For vibrancy, I mixed throw pillows of the bold-colored upholstery found in seating arrangements of the adjoining space. The flowers appear to come down from the painting to the center table bouquet. My goal was to create an atmosphere of elegance and serenity. The end result is interior spaces that give new life to the lush colors of the earth, the flowers and the traditions of Mexico."

*Juan Domingo Leaño Reyes, Turbana, S.A. de C.V.*
*Bajada de las Aguilas #299, Col. Lomas del Valle, 45110 Zapopan, Jal., Mexico*
*Tel.: (52) 3-642-3828, Fax: (52) 3-642-9810*

*Photography: Alejandro Lopez*

# *Sarah Tomerlin Lee*

Sarah Tomerlin Lee is presently the president of Tom Lee Interiors, a division of the distinguished architectural firm, Beyer Blinder Belle. She began her career writing editorials for *Vogue*, and later became the managing editor of *Harpers' Bazaar*, finishing this high fashion phase as vice president in charge of creativity at Lord & Taylor. She stepped over into interior design as the editor-in-chief of *House Beautiful* – her 'training' was observing her husband's remarkable hotels (The Four Seasons, the Plaza, the Inn on the Park, etc.). At his untimely death in 1971, she undertook the completion of his contracts and began a new career. Mrs. Lee has designed the interiors for the Parker Meridien, the New York Hilton, The Dorals, as well as many of America's great historic hotels – the Bellevue, the Willard and the Helmsley Palace.

"The Barrymore Room, atop Philadelphia's beloved Bellevue, is regarded as the most romantic room in town for tea-dancing, cocktails and weddings. The arched windows are swathed in clear pastel silk, silvered chairs and love-seats are covered with fabric with ropes of pearls, and feather motifs straight out of the fabulous thirties. The Philadelphia Library Lounge, once a store-room, now houses over two thousand books on historic Philadelphia. The dark wood paneling, the books, the comfortable chairs and couches, the portrait and the working fireplace give the atmosphere of an elegant private club."

*Sarah Tomerlin Lee, Beyer Blinder Belle/Tom Lee Interiors*
*41 East 11th Street, 2nd Floor, New York, New York 10003*
*Tel.: (212) 777-7800, Fax: (212) 475-7424*

# Heinz-Werner Maden, BDIA

Heinz-Werner Maden began his studies at the Akademie der bildenden Künste in Stuttgart and received his Master's in Interior Architecture in 1977. After winning a design competition in 1977, he founded his own firm, Geplan Design GmbH, Innenarchitektur. Being successful with numerous interior designs for the Hilton, Mövenpick and Sheraton hotel chains throughout Europe, Mr. Maden became in demand as a specialist in hotel and restaurant design. His works can be seen in such cosmopolitan cities as Brussels, Essen, Frankfurt, Funchal, Laussane, Lisbon, London, Munich and Zurich. As a member of the Association of German Interior Architects (BDIA) and the Chamber of Architects in Baden-Württemberg, he serves as a consultant for various cities' officials. Mr. Maden has designed new interior concepts for senior-living and health resorts, such as the Vital Hotel Royal pictured here. Several of his latest projects have been published in numerous magazines.

"Designing the Vital Hotel Royal in Seefeld/Tyrol, Austria, was a difficult but exciting experience, as I was engaged to design the interior of this hotel only ten months before its opening. Other Austrian designers had been unable to satisfy the wish of the owner and manager to create an extraordinary and healthy-minded resort hotel in the Austrian Alps with all the necessary recreational installations to serve as both a clinic and hotel. Against the local expectations of designing the interior in the typical regional, heavy-wooden fashion, I did just the opposite. An elegant, colorful, light but charming, warm atmosphere with a southern touch reflects the perfect ambience. The atmosphere is ideal for the holistic medicine that is offered to all the guests of this hotel. Besides the beautiful ambience, I used almost all natural materials in the interiors. For example, I installed an electric, current-free sleep area, contributing to a healthy atmosphere in the rooms. The hotel recently has been chosen as one of the best in Austria, specifically because of its interior design."

*Heinz-Werner Maden, BDIA, Geplan Design, GmbH*
*Hauptstraße 78 A, 70563 Stuttgart, Germany*
*Tel.: (49) 711-734-063, Fax: (49) 711-733-582*

*Photography: Wolfgang Schumann*

# Midori Manabe

In her thirty-year career, Midori Manabe has designed interiors for Japan's leading corporations and hotels. After receiving her Bachelor of Fine Arts degree from the Chouinard Art Institute in Los Angeles, she apprenticed at John Lautner Architects before returning to Tokyo to open her own design firm in 1972. Along with offices and hotels, Ms. Manabe's projects include country clubs, showrooms, model homes, restaurants and residences. Her expertise and talent are apparent in her myriad designs that match the needs of each client. Her client list includes Boeing Japan, Burlington Northern International Services, Ford Motor Company (Japan) Ltd. and Morrison & Foerster.

Ms. Manabe has also designed the interiors for the Hotel New Grand in Yokohama, the Tomei Country Club in Shizuoka and the Chiyoda Country Club in Ibaragi, along with private residences for Japan's leading executives. For the past fifteen years, Ms. Manabe has been in charge of the renovation of the Imperial Hotel's one thousand guest rooms.

"The grand Imperial Hotel, located in Tokyo, is the oldest hotel in Japan. The Park Suite, pictured here, is one of the hotel's major suites, located in the majestic main building. For the interior of the suite, I chose to fashion the room based on the traditional style, since a classic design will stay forever. The suite is designed to enhance the warmth, elegance and comfort to welcome its many guests from all over the world.

"My objective in the design of this suite was to obtain the perfect blend of colors, furnishings and accessories that complement and enhance each other. I chose the main color schemes of blue and peach, and incorporated them into all the furniture and accent pieces. A soft peach color serves as a backdrop to the dominant blues of the furnishings. The walls are painted a light peach to match the carpeting and draperies. The subdued color provides contrast for the furnishings in the room. Two large arm chairs, decorated with a navy flower pattern, accentuate the light blue in the sofa, while amplifying its peach colors. The room serves as a tranquil resting place for its guests. Therefore, I chose to leave the walls unadorned, except for the simple wall mirror placed above the dining room console. The room comes together as a cohesive whole, each item specially placed and decorated for the discriminate guest."

*Midori Manabe, ASID, Manabe Midori Interior Design Co., Ltd.*
*Big Tree Bldg., 7F, 2-8-6, Ebisu-Nishi, Shibuya-ku, Tokyo, Japan 150*
*Tel.: (81) 3-3464-7501, Fax: (81) 3-3464-7590*

*Photography: Ryuzo Tanabe*

# Yorgos Maryelis

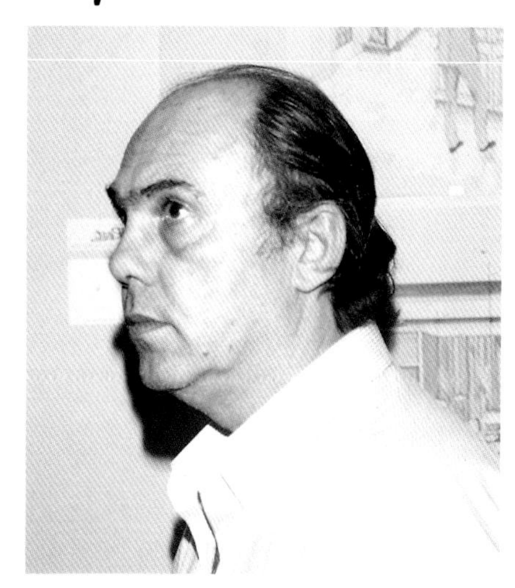

As principal designer of Maryelis & Associates in Athens, Greece, Yorgos Maryelis specializes in the design of offices, hotels and restaurants, as well as the interior design of commercial liners and cruise ships.

"This project is located along the Greek national highway leading from Patras to Athens. With its location along a major travel route, this expansive room is, of course, visited by a great number of tourists journeying the Greek coast along the Mediterranean. Because of this, I wanted to let the natural sunlight and the native colors of Greece dominate the design palette. Although this area is quite vast, with several large and open spaces, I was able to incorporate a definite feeling of cohesiveness into the design, creating a sense of consistency throughout this expansive area. As I had designed, the entire area is bathed in a generous amount of daylight, which shines through the glass paneled walls and is also filtered through the ceiling with the use of large skylights. This natural brightness radiates gently throughout the space, softly reflecting on the marble floor and bringing life and energy to the area's numerous plants and flowers. The overall result gives travelers a pleasant touch of the sun during their meal, and a place for a calm rest before the continuation of their journey."

*Yorgos Maryelis, Maryelis & Associates*
*1 Koumanoudi Street, 11474 Athens, Greece*
*Tel.: (30) 1-642-7837, Fax: (30) 1-645-5026*

# Ahmed Nour

After completing his B.Sc. in Architecture from the Faculty of Fine Arts Architectural in Cairo, Ahmed Nour began his career in Kuwait. In 1977 he expanded his business, ASA Consultants, to his home town of Cairo. Mr. Nour has designed residential projects, shopping malls, offices and hotels throughout Egypt and Kuwait. In addition to the hotel complex featured here, the Kuwait Meridien Hotel, other recent projects by ASA Consultants include the Marriott Hurgada Red Sea – Egypt.

"Located on the top floor of the Meridien Hotel in Kuwait, this pool and health club was part of a project of huge proportions. The five star hotel includes four hundred rooms and suites, a nine-hundred-person ballroom, three restaurants, a business center, and a full floor of executive suites. Because I was also designing the adjoining Salhia Shopping Mall at the same time, I was able to use the limited size of the site to maximum advantage."

---

*Ahmed Nour, ASA Consultants*
*8 Sebaweh El Masry Street, Nasser City, Cairo, Egypt*
*Tel.: (20) 2-262-7877, Fax: (20) 2-262-4163*

# Eui-Jo Oh

During his twenty years as an interior designer and architect, Eui-Jo Oh's works have ranged from residential to commercial and hospitality projects. Since 1985, Mr. Oh has served as president and principal designer of Artiplan Company, Limited, headquartered in Seoul. His projects include the Provincial Governor's Public Halls in Busan City and Chunrabuk-Do, and the interior design of the World Trade Center Korea.

"The Trad Club, a men's fashion complex, was designed to provide the total fashion experience. The basement and first and second floors are designated for retail shops, catering to the elite, well-dressed businessman. The second floor, pictured here, consists exclusively of traditional European suits mixed with American Ivy League-style fashions. In line with the sophisticated look of the goods being featured, the room's decor had to match the traditional elegance of the clothing. I chose to use rich mahogany woods and imported marble tile as major elements in this room's design. The mahogany wall units were specially designed to supply ample space and easy access to the clothing. Numerous spotlights accentuate the fine clothing and European-style paintings. The remaining four floors of this building consist of office suites, which overlook the indoor garden located next to the basement bar and restaurant. This space is planned to secure customers by providing various facilities and consulting about fashion trends."

*Eui-Jo Oh, Artiplan Company, Limited*
*794-8 Hannam-Dong Yongsan-Gu, Seoul 140, Korea*
*Tel.: (82) 2-795-1157, 2-795-1158, Fax: (82) 2-795-0773*

*Photography: Houng-Kuk Chun*

TASA

# Joshua Jih Pan, FAIA

Joshua Pan has dedicated his career in the search for a successful synthesis of eastern cultural tradition with modern western disciplines. Born in China, educated in Taiwan and the United States, he is a modernist and his works reflect his belief that design must be contextual, cohesive, harmonious and innovative. In recognition to the success of this approach, Mr. Pan has won numerous design awards from municipal, provincial and national governments, as well as the Fellow's honor bestowed by the American Institute of Architects. He also taught architectural design at two universities for thirteen years, motivating some five hundred students, with over one hundred continuing their graduate studies in the United States. Mr. Pan has served as a guest speaker and lecturer at professional conferences in Germany, Singapore, Malaysia and Korea, and was awarded the Gordon Brown Lectureship at Hong Kong University School of Architecture.

"TASA Construction Company accepted our suggestion to use its corporate color of red as the main design theme for their offices. With this in mind, they also embraced the philosophy that 'a red cloud overhead symbolizes happiness and prosperity.' This allowed us to design an office that was professional and dynamic while working within space and height limitations. The office area is over three thousand square feet and has extremely low ceilings. Our design approach was to emphasize the ceilings' height not only physically, but also psychologically by utilizing the strong and powerful color of red in the main circulation corridor. The general offices are painted in a simple white color in order to provide relief from the dominating low ceilings, and to obtain a strong visual contrast."

*Joshua Jih Pan, FAIA, J.J. Pan & Partners*
*21, Alley 12, Lane 118, Ren Ai Road, Sec. 3, Taipei, Taiwan*
*Tel.: (886) 2-701-2617, Fax: (886) 2-700-4489*

*Photography: Y.C. Chien*

# *Ed Poole, AIA, RAIA*

Architect and interior designer Ed Poole graduated from the Illinois Institute of Technology with a Bachelor's degree in Architecture in 1983. After working with several top firms in Chicago, Australia and Singapore, Mr. Poole opened his own firm, Poole Associates Private Limited, in Singapore in 1991. As its director, the company has designed contract, commercial, residential and retail interiors throughout the United States, Singapore, Australia, Malaysia, Indonesia, Hong Kong and Thailand. A Professional Member of the American Institute of Architects, Mr. Poole also holds professional memberships with the Royal Australian Institute of Architects and the Singapore Institute of Architects. "Our experience and expertise range from large commercial building design to the smallest interior details for retail shops," Mr. Poole explains about his company's philosophy. "Always paying close attention to function and detail, each project is analyzed to satisfy our clients' economic and image concerns. We do not adhere to a particular design style. Final solutions evolve from the many factors relating to a project, each viewed from a fresh perspective."

"Dynamic design and sporting motifs reinforce the young and energetic corporate image of Singapore's Royal Sporting House Pte Ltd. Tennis ball felt contrasts with a rich venetian plaster wall rendered in the client's corporate blue. The Golf Meeting Room depicts two sides of golf: the traditional detailing of clubhouses and the high performance materials used in the manufacture of clubs."

*Ed Poole, AIA, RAIA, SIA, Poole Associates Private Limited*
*209 South Bridge Road, Third Floor, Republic of Singapore 0105*
*Tel.: (65) 221-7217, Fax: (65) 221-8024*

*Photography: Seow Cheong Heng*

# Carlos Profet, ADIAA

Aruban interior designer Carlos A. Profet, born in 1955, received a Dutch education in Aruba and Holland. Mr. Profet studied interior design at the CE-Art Academy in Bogota, receiving a B.F.A. Degree. After a year of free-lancing in Aruba and Curacao, he studied environmental design at Parsons School of Design in New York City, receiving another B.F.A. Degree in 1982.

Since 1983, Mr. Profet has been owner and director of Inarch N.V. As a commercial and residential interior designer, his numerous projects include offices and banking facilities, retail spaces, condominiums and casinos throughout the Caribbean Islands.

"The Seaport Casino at the Seaport Village in Oranjestad was a massive renovation project. The scope and desire of my clients gave me the opportunity to design an interior that converted this lackluster room into a fresh, colorful and fun-filled casino. The existing dull, square columns were transformed into large, spectacular, neon-leaved palm trees. The purple and green 'trees' multiply themselves in the mirrored beams and ceiling, creating an even more fabulous scenario.

"Additional elements in the casino added to the tropical theme of the room. Colorful, hand-carved, green and orange chandeliers, resembling pineapple tops, were chosen for their whimsical effect. For vibrance, I painted the ceilings in light shades of purple to match the 'trunks' of the palm trees. For brightness, I lined the mirrored beams with bright neon lights, similar to the 'leaves' of the trees. And for the final detail, a specially designed carpet, with a tropical jungle parrots pattern, was added to complete the desired illusion."

*Carlos A. Profet, ADIAA, Inarch N.V.*
*Vondellaan 19-B, Oranjéstad, Aruba*
*Tel.: (297) 8-25677, Fax: (297) 8-32574*

*Photography: Fernando Rafael Luidens*

HAYWIRE
25¢

# Chavivan Rujimora

Chavivan Rujimora received her Bachelor's degree in Fine Arts from Bangkok's Silpakorn University in 1973. She joined Design 103 Ltd. in 1979, and has been its project manager since 1985. Her numerous design projects include a wide array of offices, service apartments, clubhouses and private residences throughout Thailand.

"Classic style and elegance were the themes chosen for the executive dining room and its adjoining lounge of the Siam Silos & Drying Company. Located in Bangkok's exclusive Ploenchit Tower, the building's architecture was also designed by Design 103 Ltd. For the decor, we chose to simplify extravagant traditional details to lessen formality and to create contemporary aesthetics and comfort. The ceiling was purposely raised to emphasize grandeur. Moldings on the ceiling and walls, belonging to the same family of detail, blend together beautifully with the wall panels. The impressive twenty-person dining table, made from rich wood, highlights the dark color of the moldings, while the white quilted-fabric chairs blend nicely with the walls and ceiling. A double glass door framed in marble and rich brass connects the dining room to the lounge. Numerous large brown arm chairs and glass tables are positioned around the room to allow for easy conversation. A tan carpet and white patterned marbles were then placed in the lounge to bring out the colors of the vases and furnishings. The warm color scheme of the dining space symbolizes propriety, while the more subdued tone of the lounge offers intimacy. Period art pieces, strategically placed, add to the completeness of the decor."

*Chavivan Rujimora, Design 103 Ltd.*
*7th-9th, 14/F, Asoke Towers Office Building, 219 Asoke Road, Bangkok 10110, Thailand*
*Tel.: (66) 2-260-0160, Fax: (66) 2-259-0489, 2-259-1191*

*Photography: Thakerng Pringpuangkeo*

# Yozo Shibata, JIA

As president of Kanko Kikaku Sekkeisha, Yozo Shibata & Associates, Yozo Shibata has completed hundreds of major hotel and restaurant installations throughout Asia. During his thirty-year career in architectural and interior design, he has worked on projects in Japan, Singapore, Malaysia, Thailand, China, Sri Lanka and Turkey. Mr. Shibata's skill and mastery in hotel architecture and design is highly appraised by developers and hotel management corporations. His major hotel projects include the Four Seasons Hotel 'Chinzanso' in Tokyo, Swissotel's 'The Bosphorus' in Istanbul, the Beijing Shangri-La Hotel, the Hilton International Colombo in Sri Lanka and the Bangkok Shangri-La Hotel in Thailand.

"Our plan for the Atrium of Japan's Haneda Air Terminal employed a new design concept: that this terminal should be a place for people to enjoy dining, meeting and relaxing, rather than being a space that people simply rush through. This expansive six-story project includes twelve restaurants and bars and fifteen retail shops located in the center of this eight hundred forty meter terminal building. Our goal in the design of the atrium was to make the space brilliant and impressive.We created an open floor design, with a glass-box elevator, to lure patrons to the concessions on the upper levels. The four round, grooved-designed marble columns travel the length of the atrium, making the space appear as one complete entity. We selected materials that were attractive, durable and easy to maintain. Terrazzo tiles line the floor, painted steel details the walls, and granite is used in the fountain. The dark granite attracts attention to the beautifully-lighted fountain with its stunning bronze statue located in the center of the atrium. This striking space is both elegant and efficient."

*Yozo Shibata, JIA, Kanko Kikaku Sekkeisha, Yozo Shibata & Associates*
*No. 17 Mori-Building, Toranomon 1-26-5, Minato-Ku, Tokyo 105, Japan*
*Tel.: (81) 3-3507-0376, Fax: (81) 3-3507-0386*

MIKIMOTO

# *Vipwal Singhakowin*

A 1975 graduate of Thailand's Silpakorn University, Vipwal Singhakowin joined Design 103 Ltd. in 1984, becoming one of the firm's most capable interior designers. In addition to the design of the Chalermkrung Royal Theatre, pictured here, her major works include IBM Thailand's ten thousand square meter office, The Old Siam Plaza shopping complex and the renovation of the Siam Centre in Thailand.

"The Chalermkrung Royal Theatre was a gift bestowed by King Rama VII to the Thai people in 1933 to commemorate the 150th Anniversary of the City of Bangkok. The original architect, Prince Samaichalerm Kritakara, fused traditional Thai spirit with art deco to create a memorable venue for the performing arts. For the renovation of this auditorium by Design 103 Ltd., set on a preserved historical site, we chose to bring contemporary detail to the traditional Thai design. Columns and ceiling beams were left exposed to fully express their structural meaning. We added decor which would enhance these existing features, while following the mannerism of the traditional architecture. In keeping with the 'East meets West' concept, an Oriental palette was used, incorporating sparkling gold prosceniums, decorative motifs and vibrant red curtains, seating and carpeting. A softer touch of purple and gold Thai silk lines the walls. Elaborate antique gilded woodwork and art objects were then restored and repositioned on the ceiling, gallery, railings and doors. The most distinctive pieces in this auditorium are the Three Revered Gods of Thai performing arts, placed prominently above the stage. The ceiling-level linear houselights were given a new multi-colored dimension, operating rhythmically, and creating a whimsical touch. With a capacity for seven hundred people, the hall was then equipped with state-of-the-art stage lighting, sound, seating and special effects, including advanced equipment which facilitates as many as twenty scene changes."

*Vipwal Singhakowin, Design 103 Ltd.*
*7th-9th, 14/F, Asoke Towers Office Building, 219 Asoke Road, Bangkok 10110, Thailand*
*Tel.: (66) 2-260-0160, Fax: (66) 2-259-0489, 2-259-1191*

*Photography: Thakerng Pringpuangkeo*

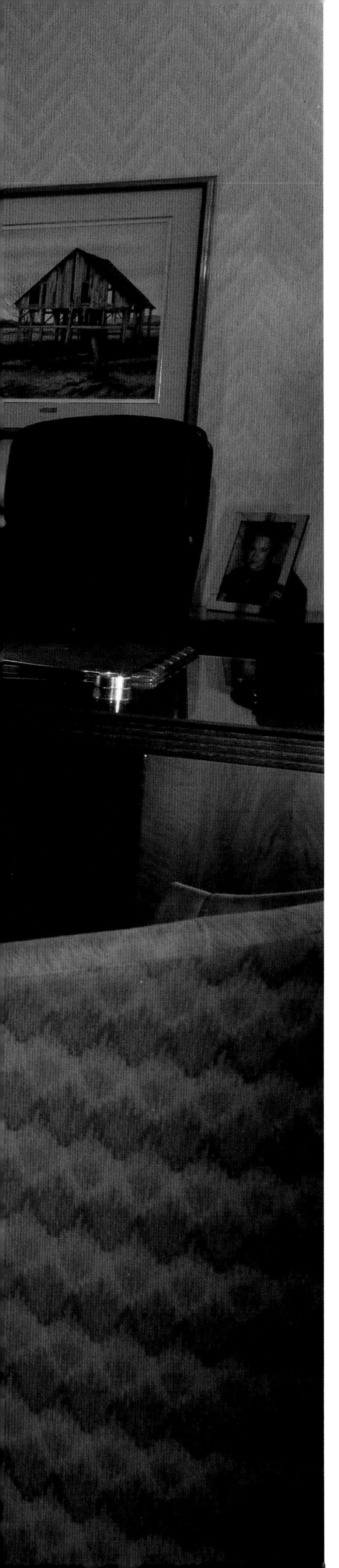

# John Wendover

John Wendover was born in Grimsby, United Kingdom, and emigrated to Canada in 1952. He graduated in Decorative Arts (Licence ès Arts) with honors from McGill University. In 1984, he opened his own design company, Les Concepts Decoratifs Wendover, Inc. in Montreal. Mr. Wendover's principal works include upscale residences and executive suites with extensive art collections, government collection displays and museums, and the authentication of works from antiquity.

"My client, a prominent orthopaedic surgeon, wanted an inviting look for his office, rather than that of a sterile medical office. I accomplished this by maximizing the interplay between the earth-tone walls, the bold and massive oak desk, the warmth of the sequoia wall units and contemporary art. The modern environment is balanced by the use of an antique Chinese screen, which also serves as a discrete separation from the examination area. For the waiting room and reception area, warm colors were used. The whole environment is accented by contemporary art as well as classic and modern forms in the blend of different woods and styles in the furnishings. The soothing nature of the clinic is further enhanced by the presence of tropical plants."

*John Wendover, B.A. (Hon.), Les Concepts Decoratifs Wendover, Inc.*
*3875 Saint-Urban, Suite 611, Montreal, Quebec, Canada H2W 1V1*
*Tel.: (514) 281-2073, Fax: (514) 844-8843, (514) 769-5618*

*Photography: José Bouthillette*

# Gaby Widajanti, IAI

International exposure to the profession of interior design came early to Gaby Widajanti as she pursued her education. After studying Architecture at Tarumanegara University, she traveled to Berlin's Technishe University where she graduated with honors in 1977. Ms. Widajanti gained experience in a variety of areas in her first position with Bent Severin, Singapore, where she was given responsibility for design coordination, office management, and marketing and presentation. In 1985 she started her own interior design firm in Jakarta, Ahara Prima Design, Pt.

Ever-aware of the need to bring contemporary, efficient design proposals to her commercial clients, Ms. Widajanti has availed herself of numerous professional seminars and workshops in England, the United States, Taiwan, Singapore and Germany. Her commitment to bringing quality, creativity and style to her projects has helped to make her firm successful and sought after by clients throughout Indonesia. Ms. Widajanti is a member of two professional associations, Ikatan Arsitek Indonesia and Himpunan Design Interior Indonesia.

"Professional, contemporary yet unadorned were the main objectives in designing this reception and lounge area for Modern Bank in Jakarta, Indonesia. The sweeping, curved counter is a refreshing departure from the straight, rigid counters seen in other offices. I used marble on both the counters and the floor to blend the two surfaces.

"With the focus of the room on the counters and office area, ceiling lights shine downward, spotlighting the area while highlighting the marble's brightness. The dark mahogany diamond accentuates the dark specks of the floor's marble and marks the center point of the room. Although the design utilizes straight lines, the circle placed at the center carries on the same circular theme I used in the counter. I selected the dark color from the diamond design and incorporated it in the room's design – in the window and wall moldings and chairs.

"Comfortable leather chairs placed against the walls divert one's eyes to the beautiful peacock painting hung behind the counter. The bird's colorful feathers provide vibrance and radiance to the room. I used the firm's corporate color, turquoise, throughout the space, in the paneling, columns and chair backs. While the area is professional and efficient, it is also comfortable and understated."

*Gaby Widajanti, HDII, IAI, Ahara Prima Design Pt. Interior Design*
*Jl. Birah II No. 4, Kebayoran Baru, Jakarta 12180, Indonesia*
*Tel.: (62) 21-712-388, Fax: (62) 21-720-7432*

*Photography: Rudi Sugiharto*

# Evan Michael Williams

Both an architect and interior designer, Evan Michael Williams brings impressive credentials to his commercial, residential, hotel and restaurant design projects. Born in Kingston, Jamaica, Mr. Williams attended Pratt Institute in New York, and his Bachelor's Degree in Architecture prepared him for his highly successful career throughout the Caribbean. His expertise has merited high accolades from his peers, and he has received several distinguished awards including the Governor General's Award for Excellence in Architecture, the Silver Musgrave Centenary Medal, and the Jamaica 21 Award for Excellence in Architecture. Evan Williams is the principal of Design Collaborative, Architects and DCI International, Interior Designers, both in Jamaica. Design Collaborative International has associated offices in London, United Kingdom; New York, United States; Bogota, Colombia; Bridgetown, Barbados; Castries, St. Lucia; and Port of Spain, Trinidad.

"The Sandals La Toc in St. Lucia is the latest addition to the Caribbean chain of all-inclusive hotels operated by Sandals Resorts International. The property, formerly owned and operated by Cunard, underwent a US$20 million renovation that was completed in March of 1993. Among the many public areas which I was asked to design was the Main Pavilion Restaurant. This structure formed the centerpiece of the Central Facilities Area. My client's main concern was the integration of the lobby, located at the upper level, and views of the Caribbean, while introducing the specialty restaurant, at the lower level, to arriving guests. The rather simple solution was influenced by the temples of ancient Greece, found along the Mediterranean Coast. The drama of space is enhanced by the room being surrounded by the largest swimming pool in the eastern Caribbean. Upon entering the main lobby, one is immediately drawn to the framed view of the Caribbean Sea, framed by two columns originating from the lower level. The soaring pyramid space, forty-eight feet high at its apex, evokes a spirituality in its grandeur and luxury."

*Evan Michael Williams, DCI International Interior Designers*
*19 Surbiton Road, Kingston 10, Jamaica, West Indies*
*Tel.: (809) 926-4288; Fax: (809) 929-2007*

# Jaci Yoap, IFDA

After twenty-five years in the design profession, Jaci Yoap is continually studying and traveling in order to expand her knowledge and inventory of fine furniture and works of art. A specialist in blending Oriental, Victorian and French designs. Ms. Yoap also lectures on the arts and customs of China and on various other design topics.

"The Hunt Library is the latest design vignette for this specialty furniture store, Simply Charming, located in the historic waterfront district on Lake Michigan. The area pictured here features European and American antiques, such as the black hunter statue, the vibrant leopard wall hanging and various sized vases. The room also displays pieces from my own intricate Rosewood Designs Collection. The rosewood arch serves as a natural divider between the two display rooms, one showcasing my Rosewood Collection and the other exhibiting French furniture. Other Rosewood Collection pieces pictured here include the tables, chairs, buffet and curios."

*Jaci Yoap, IFDA, Interiors by Jaci*
*Highway B, Pound, Wisconsin 54161*
*Tel.: (414) 897-3536, Fax: (414) 897-2825*

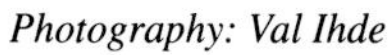

*Photography: Val Ihde*

# Hugh Zimmern

Hugh Zimmern serves many different capacities in the Leigh & Orange Ltd. group of companies. As the principal director and partner of its main office in Hong Kong, he is also managing director of its Thailand office. A British native, Mr. Zimmern received his formal education in architecture and Master's degree from Edinburgh University in Scotland. Mr. Zimmern is a member of the Royal Institute of British Architects and the Hong Kong Institute of Architects. A recipient of the Sir Robert Lorimer Award, the HKIA President's Prize and the Pace Designer Award, Mr. Zimmern's projects span the Asian continent. A partial list of his major works include the Seri Centre, AT&T offices and Nai Lert Building in Bangkok, the Pavilion Resorts in Pranburi, the Inya Lake Hotel in Yangon, the Ritz-Carlton Hotel in Hong Kong, and the Mandarin Oriental Hotel and 37 Le Duan Street in Saigon.

"Michelle's Restaurant is set on the first floor of an ice store originally designed by Leigh & Orange in the 1930's. The theme of a slightly decayed Mediterranean villa gone awry is extended to the design of the chairs and light fittings. Nothing in this restaurant fits the traditional mode: not the violin-back chairs with large, exaggerated cushions, the spotlight chandeliers, the art pieces or even the wine rack. Rather than select paintings to adorn the walls, I turned one wall into a painting with a large mural portrait. The other walls are finished in pure pigment with a wax finish, while cornices are redone in an antiqued metal leaf. This unique restaurant in the heart of Hong Kong has the inviting and intimate air of an Italian *palazzo*."

*Hugh Zimmern, Leigh & Orange Ltd.*
*3rd Floor, Chung Shun Building, 88 Hing Fat Street, Causeway Bay, Hong Kong*
*Tel.: (852) 806-1312, Fax: (852) 806-0343*

*Photography: Mark Atkinson*

*fin.*

*Indexes . . .*

# *Indexes*

***Designers Index:*** Whether for a private residence or for a commercial project, selecting the right interior designer is rarely an easy choice. To assist you with your decision, this book has been specially edited to act as a portfolio illustrating the finest work of a wide range of the world's leading interior designers.

On the preceding pages, you have had the opportunity to see each designer and to learn about their backgrounds and qualifications. You have been able to see their favorite design projects and read each designer's explanation of how they rose to the challenges each project presented. If this book has been successful, you probably have at least one designer in mind to interview for your upcoming interior design project. After selecting a designer offering the right style, the right look, and the right design philosophy, the next question usually concerns fees and payment structures.

On the following pages, each of the participating designers has provided contact information, a listing of their design specializations, and a general idea of their design fees. Almost all of the designers featured in this edition work internationally, and all have agreed to provide immediate attention to inquiries from readers of this book. You probably already know which of these one hundred designers is the best for you – and all it takes now is a simple phone call to make *your* design project that designer's new favorite!

***Photographers Index:*** For the professional designer or architect, this book doubles as an international portfolio of the world's best interior and architectural photographers. The preceding pages have featured the finest examples of their work, and you are now invited to use the following index to locate and contact these professionals for projects throughout the world. Each index listing includes the photographer's name, company, address, telephone and fax numbers, as well as the pages on which their work appears. Whether your projects are in North America, Asia, South America, Europe or the Middle East, this index is a convenient contact directory of qualified interior and architectural photographers virtually anywhere in the world.

# Designers Index

***Jack Adams, ASID***
Adams Design, Inc.
1415 Kalakaua Avenue, Suite 204
Honolulu, Hawaii 96826
Tel.: (808) 955-6100, Fax: (808) 947-4311
Residential, hotel and restaurant interior design.
Fee structure: available upon request.
*Pages 80-81*

***Anita-Louise Aiello, ARIDO, ASID***
Design Concepts
5045 Orbiter Drive
Building 12, Suite 400
Mississauga, Ontario, Canada L4W 4Y4
Tel.: (905) 602-7075, Fax: (905) 602-7073
Residential, office, hotel, restaurant and contract interior design.
Fee structure: hourly consultation fee structured to size of project.
*Pages 18-19*

***Jun Alday***
Jun Alday Limited
19-D, Portfield Building, 10 Yuk Sau Street
Happy Valley, Hong Kong
Tel.: (852) 573-5529, Fax: (852) 838-2312
Residential, corporate and hotel suites interior design.
Fee structure: available upon request.
*Pages 126-127*

***Dale Anderson, ASID***
Dale Carol Anderson Ltd.
2030 North Magnolia Avenue
Chicago, Illinois 60614
Tel.: (312) 348-5200, Fax: (312) 348-5271
Residential interior design.
Fee structure: project specific.
*Pages 20-21*

***Nancy J. Anderson, ASID***
Nancy J. Anderson Interiors
3065 Clay Street
San Francisco, California 94115
Tel.: (415) 346-5022, (800) 484-9971 x. 5022,
Fax: (415) 346-1554
Residential interior design.
Fee structure: available upon request.
*Pages 82-83*

***Samir Badro***
Green Line Company, Ltd.
Post Office Box 5835
Sharjah, United Arab Emirates
Tel.: (971) 6-333-731, Fax: (971) 6-332-650

Green Line Company
P.O. Box 9227
Dubai, United Arab Emirates
Tel.: (971) 4-313-563, Fax: (971) 4-310-574

Green Line Company
Sheikh Suroor Bin Mohammad Al Nahyan Building
Corniche Road
Abu Dhabi, United Arab Emirates
Tel.: (971) 2-656-533, Fax: (971) 2-656-662

G.L. Interiors, W.L.L.
Tayar Center, P.O. Box 55066
Sin El Fil, Beirut, Lebanon
Tel.: (961) 1-500-866, Fax: (961) 1-492-599

G.L. Syria Ltd.
Al Abbaseen Square, Bshara Al Khoury Street
P.O. Box 7615
Damascus, Syria
Tel.: (963) 11-334-162, Fax: (963) 11-247-780

Green Line Inc. (Le Coin)
115 South Robertson Boulevard
Los Angeles, California 90048, USA
Tel.: (310) 274-8413, Fax: (310) 247-1601

GLM Corporation
2665 South Bayshore Drive, Suite 600
Miami, Florida 33133, USA
Tel.: (305) 858-8080, Fax: (305) 854-6064

G.L. Company Limited
150 Brompton Road, Knightsbridge
London SW3 1HZ, United Kingdom
Tel.: (44) 71-581-7034, Fax: (44) 71-584-0659

G.L. Co. France
1 Rond Point Des Champs Elysees
Paris 75008, France
Tel.: (33) 1-42-89-20-90, Fax: (33) 1-42-89-20-56

G.L. Co.
Via Meichiorre, Gioia 41
Milano, Italy
Tel.: (39) 2-66-98-42-01, Fax: (39) 2-67-00-482

G.L. Interiors Pte. Ltd.
391 A, Orchard Road
Ngee Ann City, Tower A, # 17-09
Singapore
Tel.: (65) 738-6665, Fax: (65) 738-6667
Residential and commercial architectural and interior design.
Fee structure: varies according to project.
*Pages 128-129*

***Tapati Dali Basu, ASID***
Complete Interior Design
46 Ferncliff Drive
West Hartford, Connecticut 06117
Tel.: (203) 232-9713
Residential, office, contract, hotel and restaurant interior design.
Fee structure: available upon request.
*Pages 22-23*

***Samuel Botero***
Samuel Botero Associates, Inc.
150 East 58th Street
New York, New York 10155
Tel.: (212) 935-5155, Fax: (212) 832-0714
Residential, hotel and restaurant interior design.
Fee structure: design fee average US$1,200.00 per room, plus retail on items purchased, 25% on construction; set fee upon request depending on scope of project.
*Inside flyleaf, pages 3, 5, 24-25*

***Geoffrey N. Bradfield, ASID***
Jay Spectre, Inc.
964 Third Avenue
New York, New York 10022
Tel.: (212) 758-1773, Fax: (212) 688-1571
Residential and office interior design.
Fee structure: available upon request.
*Front cover, pages 2, 4, 26-27, back cover*

***Fernando Braverman***
Arquiconceptos Instalaciones, SA de CV
Campos Eliseos 188-402, Col. Polanco
11560 Mexico DF, Mexico
Tel.: (52) 5-280-9198, 5-280-9573
Fax: (52) 5-281-1320
Residential and office interior design.
Fee structure: available upon request.
*Pages 130-131*

***Alfredo Brito***
Brito Interior Design, Inc.
1000 Quayside Terrace, Suite 412
Miami, Florida 33138
Tel.: (305) 895-8539
Residential, hotel and restaurant interior design.
Fee structure: initial design fee plus retail for furniture, fabrics, accessories and antiques.
*Pages 16-17, 28-29*

***Kathleen Buoymaster***
Kathleen Buoymaster, Inc.
6933 La Jolla Boulevard
La Jolla, California 92037
Tel.: (619) 456-2850, Fax: (619) 456-0672
Residential interior design.
Fee structure: available upon request.
*Pages 84-85*

***Ruth Burt***
236 East 82nd Street, Suite 3D
New York, New York 10028
Tel.: (212) 737-7507, Fax: (212) 472-7782
Residential interior design.
Fee structure: available upon request.
*Pages 30-31*

***Olivier-Clement Cacoub***
Architecte en Chef des Batiments Civils et Palais Nationaux
54, avenue d'Iena, 75116 Paris, France
Tel.: (33) 1-47-20-08-23, Fax: (33) 1-47-20-42-58

88, avenue d'Iena, 75116 Paris, France
Tel.: (33) 1-47-20-35-49, Fax: (33) 1-47-23-65-81
Residential, office, government contracts, hotel and restaurant interior design.
Fee structure: varies according to project, available upon request.
*Pages 162-163*

***Barbara Jean Campbell, ASID***
Barbara Campbell Interiors
9812 Falls Road
Potomac, Maryland 20854
Tel.: (301) 983-4255, Fax: (301) 983-8836
Residential interior design.
Fee structure: design fee and sales at list.
*Pages 32-33*

***Lillian Chain, ASID***
2222 Avenue of the Stars, Suite 2501
Los Angeles, California 90067
Tel.: (310) 277-3855
Residential and office interior design.
Fee structure: varies according to project, available upon request.
*Pages 86-87*

***Juckkradej Chantrakulkasem***
Balancing Act Co., Ltd.
2044/118 Chan Road, Chngnthr.
Bangkok Dst./Yannawa, Thailand
Tel.: (66) 2-286-8795, Fax: (66) 2-392-7596
Residential, office, contract, hotel and restaurant interior design.
Fee structure: available upon request.
*Pages 132-133*

***Moon-Young Choi***
M.Y. Design Office
Han-Nam Dong 707-34, Yong-San Ku
Seoul, South Korea
Tel.: (82) 2-749-2077, Fax: (82) 2-749-2075
Hotel, restaurant, office and contract interior architecture and design.
Fee structure: Negotiable.
*Pages 164-165*

***Henry M. Conversano***
Conversano & Associates
5758 Broadway
Oakland, California 94618
Tel.: (510) 547-6890, Fax: (510) 547-3807
Hotel, casino and resort destination conceptual interior and exterior design.
Fee structure: depends on individual project.
*Pages 166-167*

***Cordelia Cortés***
Cordelia Cortés, S.A.
Paseo de las Palmas 885, 3-1-1
Col. Lomas de Chapultepec
11000 Mexico DF, Mexico
Tel.: (52) 5-520-5078, Fax: (52) 5-540-7995
Residential, office, hotel and restaurant interior design.
Fee structure: varies according to project.
*Pages 88-89*

***Antonio de Garay***
Antonio de Garay Arquitectos Asociados
Petrarca 223-204, Col. Polanco
Mexico DF 11560, Mexico
Tel.: (52) 5-250-5241, Fax: (52) 5-203-1368
Office interior design.
Fee structure: varies according to project.
*Pages 168-169*

***Floren Garcia de Saint Malo, ASID***
Post Office Box 87-3195
Panama City 7, Panama
Tel.: (507) 64-5729, 23-5108, Fax: (507) 64-1643
Residential interior design.
Fee structure: fee varies according to project.
*Pages 134-135*

***Michael de Santis, ASID***
Michael de Santis, Inc.
1110 Second Avenue
New York, New York 10022
Tel.: (212) 753-8871, Fax: (212) 935-7777
Residential and commercial interior design.
Fee structure: available upon request.
*Pages 8-9, 34-35, 224, back cover*

***Bernardo de Silva***
Vexon S.A.
Gonzalitos Sur 456
Monterrey NL 64050, Mexico
Tel.: (52) 83-335-133, Fax: (52) 83-332-288
Residential and office interior design.
Fee structure: varies according to project, available upon request.
*Pages 170-171*

***Jeanne Dipotontro, IAI***
P.T. Cipta Mustika
Jl. Let. Jend. S. Parman 78, 3rd Floor
Jakarta 11410, Indonesia
Tel.: (62) 21-567-1513, 21-567-3595
Fax: (62) 21-548-2162
Architectural and interior design.
Fee structure: available upon request.
*Pages 136-137*

***Robert Dirstein***
Dirstein Robertson Limited
77 Yorkville Avenue
Toronto, Ontario, Canada M5R 1C1
Tel.: (416) 961-6211, Fax: (416) 961-5537
Residential and contract interior design.
Fee structure: fees based on retail, plus a percentage charge on construction.
*Pages 36-37*

***Rodger Dobbel, ASID***
Rodger Dobbel Interiors
23 Vista Avenue
Piedmont, California 94611
Tel.: (510) 654-6723, Fax: (510) 658-7556
Residential interior design.
Fee structure: available upon request.
*Pages 6-7, 90-91*

***Melanie Doss, ASID***
Doss Design Associates
602 South Gay Street, Suite 102
Knoxville, Tennessee 37902
Tel.: (615) 637-4149, Fax: (615) 523-7949
Office, educational and residential interior design.
Fee structure: varies according to project, available upon request.
*Pages 172-173*

***Trudy Dujardin, ASID***
Trudy Dujardin Interiors
Post Office Box 2655 Saugatuck Station
3 Sylvan Road South
Westport, Connecticut 06880
Tel.: (203) 222-1019
Residential, office, contract and historic preservation interior design.
Fee structure: available upon request.
*Pages 38-39*

***Susanne E. Eisinger, ASID***
Interior Design Concepts
9705 Kendale Road
Potomac, MD 20854
Tel.: (301) 365-7008, Fax: (301) 469-5912
Residential and contract interior design.
Fee structure: varies according to project.
*Pages 40-41*

***Juan Jose Espiñeira Cortizas***
Anatole France No. 26, Chapultepec Polanco
Mexico DF 11560, Mexico
Tel.: (52) 281-4065, Fax: (52) 280-7259
Residential and office interior design.
Fee structure: available upon request.
*Pages 92-93*

***William R. Eubanks***
William R. Eubanks Interior Design
1516 Union Avenue
Memphis, Tennessee 38104
Tel.: (901) 272-1825, Fax: (901) 272-1845
Residential and contract interior design.
Fee structure: available upon request.
*Pages 42-43*

***Naglaa A. Farsi***
Silver Branch Boutique
Post Office Box 2525
Jeddah, Saudi Arabia 21461
Tel.: (966) 2-654-6464, Fax: (966) 2-654-9945
Residential and boutique interior design.
Fee structure: varies according to project, available upon request.
*Pages 138-139*

***Elwyn Colby Ferris***
Elwyn Colby Ferris Interior Design
1417 T Street, NW
Washington DC, 20009
Tel.: (202) 387-3161, Fax: (202) 332-8804
Residential, office, hotel and restaurant interior design.
Fee structure: available upon request.
*Pages 44-45*

***Foo Fatt Chuen***
Axis Network Sdn. Bhd.
Suite 7.15, 7th Floor
Wisma Central, Jalan Ampang
Kuala Lumpur 50450, Malaysia
Tel.: (60) 3-263-4181, Fax: (60) 3-263-4186
Hotel, restaurant and retail interior design.
Fee structure: varies according to project, available upon request.
*Pages 174-175*

***Landy Gardner***
Landy Gardner Interiors
1903 21st Avenue South
Nashville, Tennessee 37212
Tel.: (615) 383-1880, Fax: (615) 383-4167
Residential and office interior design.
Fee structure: available upon request.
*Pages 46-47*

***Marisabel Gómez de Morales***
Gómez Vázquez Aldana & Associates
Aurelio Ortega 764
Zapopan, Jalisco, Mexico
Tel.: (52) 3-656-2939, Fax: (52) 3-656-5747
Residential, office, contract, hotel and restaurant interior design.
Fee structure: available upon request.
*Pages 176-177*

***Bosco Gutierrez Cortina***
Gutierrez Cortina Arquitectos, S.C.
Av. Revolucion #1373, Col. Campestre Tlacopac
01040 Mexico DF, Mexico
Tel.: (52) 5-662-0190, Fax: (52) 5-662-9816
Residential interior design.
Fee structure: 500,000 DLLS.
*Pages 178-179*

***Kim E. Gwozdz***
Provenance
2425 East Camelback Road, Suite 450
Phoenix, Arizona 85016
Tel.: (602) 912-8552, Fax: (602) 912-8599
Residential and office interior design.
Fee structure: varies according to project.
*Pages 94-95*

***Anthony Jules Harris***
Metro Cuadrado, S.A. de C.V.
1A, Cda. de Gavilan No. 11, Col. San Miguel
Iztapalapa, Mexico DF 09360, Mexico
Tel.: (52) 5-685-7381, Fax: (52) 5-685-5706
Residential, office, hotel and restaurant interior design.
Fee structure: by project with estimate.
*Pages 96-97*

***Myriel Böes Hiner, Allied Member ASID***
Innova Interiors, Inc.
7802 Davenport Street
Omaha, Nebraska 68114
Tel.: (402) 392-1115, Fax: (402) 392-0188
Residential, hotel, restaurant, office, contract and retail interior design.
Fee structure: US$75.00-$90.00 per cost plus materials and expenses.
*Pages 78-79, 98-99*

***Bosco Ho***
B63, Provident Centre, Wharf Road
North Point, Hong Kong
Tel.: (852) 811-5733 x.670
Fax: (852) 811-5775, 811-5904
Office, hotel and restaurant interior design.
Fee structure: varies according to project, available upon request.
*Pages 180-181*

***Charles "Chip" A. Johnston, Jr., ASID, IFDA***
Chip Johnston Interiors
2996 Grandview Avenue NE, Suite 300
Atlanta, Georgia 30305
Tel.: (404) 231-4141
Residential and office interior design.
Fee structure: available upon request.
*Pages 48-49*

***Judith Sisler Johnston***
Sisler-Williams Interior Design
9143 Phillips Highway, Suite 260
Jacksonville, Florida 32256
Tel.: (904) 363-0177, Fax: (904) 363-9980
Residential, contract, health care and retirement facilities interior design; model home merchandising.
Fee structure: varies according to project.
*Pages 50-51*

***Masae Kawamura***
Kanko Kikaku Sekkeisha, Yozo Shibata & Associates
No. 17 Mori Bldg., 1-26-5 Toranomon
Minato-ku, Tokyo 105, Japan
Tel.: (81) 3-3507-0376, Fax: (81) 3-3507-0386
Hotel and restaurant interior design.
Fee structure: available upon request.
*Pages 182-183*

***Debra S. Kelley***
Kelley Designs, Inc.
30 New Orleans Road
Hilton Head Island, South Carolina 29928
Tel.: (803) 785-6911, Fax: (803) 785-6778
Residential, hotel, restaurant, office, contract and yacht interior design.
Fee structure: available upon request; varies according to project.
*Pages 52-53*

***Patricia Klee, ASID***
Post Office Box 31150
Santa Barbara, California 93130
Tel.: (805) 969-6102, Fax: (805) 969-0390
Residential and commercial interior design; design for agri-business complexes and ranches.
Fee structure: available upon request.
*Pages 100-101*

***Mehmet Konuralp***
Bostan Sok. No. 9/2
80200 Tesvikiye, Istanbul, Turkey
Tel.: (90) 212-236-1681, 212-261-2141
Fax: (90) 212-236-1680
Residential, office, hotel and restaurant interior design.
Fee structure: percentage basis on the total cost of the building, percentage varies on type and size of building.
*Pages 140-141*

***Nancy Kwok, MCSD***
Hinex Universal Design Contracting Co., Ltd.
3102, Top Glory Tower
262, Gloucester Road, Hong Kong
Tel.: (852) 833-0228, Fax: (852) 833-0223
Contract, office, hotel and restaurant interior design.
Fee structure: varies according to project.
*Pages 184-185*

***Wilfried Lachermair***
Wilfried Lachermair & Partner
Planen und Bauen GmbH
Talstr. 25, 42697 Solingen, Germany
Tel.: (49) 212-79055, Fax: (49) 212-79050
Retail fashion, boutique, shopping center, hotel and restaurant interior design.
Fee structure: varies according to project.
*Pages 186-187*

***Pat Larin, ASID***
Pat Larin Interiors
12720 Dianne Drive
Los Altos Hills, California 94022
Tel.: (415) 941-4613, Fax: (415) 941-4047
Residential and office interior design.
Fee structure: varies with type of project.
*Pages 102-103*

***Patricia A. Lazor, Allied ASID***
Patricia A. Lazor Inc.
Roebling Road
Bernardsville, New Jersey 07924
Tel.: (908) 766-4019, Fax: (908) 766-7610
Residential and office interior design.
Fee structure: available upon request.
*Pages 54-55*

***Juan Domingo Leaño Reyes***
Turbana, S.A. de C.V.
Bajada de las Aguilas No. 299
Col. Lomas del Valle
45110 Zapopan, Jal., Mexico
Tel.: (52) 3-642-3828, Fax: (52) 3-642-9810
Residential, hotel and office interior design.
Fee structure: available upon request.
*Pages 188-189*

***Sarah Tomerlin Lee***
Beyer Blinder Belle/Tom Lee Interiors
41 East 11th Street, 2nd Floor
New York, New York 10003
Tel.: (212) 777-7800, Fax: (212) 475-7424
Hotel and restaurant interior design.
Fee structure: varies according to project, available upon request.
*Pages 190-191*

***Cynthia S. Leftwich, ASID, IBD***
1711 Avenue J, Suite 108
Lubbock, Texas 79401
Tel.: (806) 747-5584, Fax: (806) 747-5586
Residential and contract interior design.
Fee structure: varies according to project.
*Pages 104-105*

***Elaine Licha, ASID***
Elaine Licha Interiors
Calle Taft No. 1, Apt. 15-E
Condado, San Juan, Puerto Rico 00911
Tel.: (809) 727-7399, 724-2070
Fax: (809) 727-7399
Residential and office interior design.
Fee structure: varies according to project.
*Pages 142-143*

***Michael Love, ASID***
Quantum Design Group
121 Madison Avenue
New York, New York 10016
Tel.: (212) 545-0301, Fax: (212) 689-4064
Residential, contract and medical office interior design.
Fee structure: depending on project: design fee for preliminary proposals, US$200 hourly charges, 40% mark-up on showroom purchases, 20% on antiques.
*Pages 13, 56-57*

***Lois E. Lugonja, ASID***
Lois Lugonja Interior Design
23515 Fernhill Drive
Los Altos Hills, California 94024
Tel.: (415) 948-3185
Residential and office interior design.
Fee structure: Hourly fee for consultation or construction supervision; retail for furnishings and fabrics.
*Pages 106-107*

***Heinz-Werner Maden, BDIA***
Geplan Design, GmbH
Hauptstraße 78 A, 70563 Stuttgart, Germany
Tel.: (49) 711-734-063, Fax: (49) 711-733-582
Hotel, restaurant and senior hotel interior design.
Fee structure: available upon request.
*Pages 192-193*

***Midori Manabe, ASID***
Manabe Midori Interior Design Co., Ltd.
Big Tree Building, 7th Floor, 2-8-6, Ebisu-Nishi
Shibuya-ku, Tokyo, Japan 150
Tel.: (81) 3-3464-7501, Fax: (81) 3-3464-7590
Interior design of residence, model homes, hotel, restaurant, club house, office and showrooms.
Fee structure: available upon request.
*Pages 194-195*

***Yorgos Maryelis***
Maryelis & Associates
1 Koumanoudi Street
11474 Athens, Greece
Tel.: (30) 1-642-7837, Fax: (30) 1-645-5026
Office, hotel and restaurant interior design, and interior design of ferries and cruise ships.
Fee structure: available upon request.
*Pages 196-197*

***Emma Matienzo-Smeal, Allied ASID***
The Design Group of Washington, ECS/AA Decor
4020 Biscayne Drive
Winter Springs, Florida 32708
Tel.: (407) 695-2500, Fax: (407) 366-3324

10108 Springlake Drive
Fairfax, Virginia 22030
Tel.: (703) 273-4466
Residential and contract interior design.
Fee structure: varies according to project.
*Pages 58-59*

***Rod Maxwell, ISID***
R.A. Maxwell, Inc.
5461 N. East River Road, Suite 901
Chicago, Illinois 60656-1130
Tel.: (312) 693-2857, Fax: (312) 693-6620
Residential interior design.
Fee structure: available upon request.
*Pages 15, 60-61*

***Ricardo Mayer, ASID***
Arquitetura e Palnejamento
680-708 Avenida Copacabana
Rio de Janeiro, Brazil 22050
Tel.: (55) 21-256-8616, Fax: (55) 21-256-8616
Residential, office, contract, hotel and restaurant interior design.
Fee structure: varies according to project; available upon request.
*Pages 144-145*

***H. Glenn McGee, AIA, ASID***
McGee-Howle & Associates, Architects, Inc.
2801 Ocean Drive, Suite 302
Vero Beach, Florida 32963
Tel.: (407) 231-4222, Fax: (407) 231-4311
Residential interior design.
Fee structure: available upon request.
*Pages 62-63*

***Carol Meltzer, ASID***
P.T.M. Interiors Unlimited Designs
107 East 60th Street
New York, New York 10022
Tel.: (212) 688-4430, 688-4708
Fax: (212) 688-4463

64345 Via Risso
Palm Springs, California 92262
Tel.: (619) 322-0702, Fax: (619) 322-6084
Residential, hotel and restaurant interior design.
Fee structure: Initial flat fee billing plus percentage of cost; initial flat fee plus hourly.
*Pages 10-11, 64-65*

***Wajih Naccache***
Design Team
Naser Street, Post Office Box 1776
Sharjah, United Arab Emirates
Tel.: (971) 6-593-035, Fax: (971) 6-597-521
Residential, hotel and restaurant interior design.
Fee structure: cost plus 25%.
*Pages 124-125, 146-147*

***Ahmed Nour***
ASA Consultants
8 Sebaweh El Masry Street
Nasser City, Cairo, Egypt
Tel.: (20) 2-262-7877, Fax: (20) 2-262-4163
Residential, office, hotel and restaurant interior design.
Fee structure: varies according to project, available upon request.
*Pages 198-199*

***Eui-Jo Oh***
Artiplan Company, Limited
794-8 Hannam-Dong Yongsan-Gu
Seoul 140, Korea
Tel.: (82) 2-795-1157, (82) 2-795-1158
Fax: (82) 2-795-0773
Residential, commercial, hotel and restaurant interior design.
Fee structure: varies according to project, available upon request.
*Pages 200-201*

***Joshua Jih Pan, FAIA***
J.J. Pan & Partners
21, Alley 12, Lane 118, Ren Ai Road, Sec. 3
Taipei, Taiwan, ROC
Tel.: (886) 2-701-2617, Fax: (886) 2-700-4489
Office, hotel and restaurant interior architecture and design.
Fee structure: 8-12% of construction cost.
*Pages 12, 202-203*

***Ed Poole, AIA, RAIA, SIA***
Poole Associates Private Limited
209 South Bridge Road, Third Floor
Republic of Singapore 0105
Tel.: (65) 221-7217, Fax: (65) 221-8024
Residential, office, hotel, restaurant and food retailer specialist interior design.
Fee structure: available upon request; varies upon scope of services, time frame and location.
*Pages 160-161, 204-205*

***Noranit Tui Pranich, ASID***
Pranich & Associates
270 South County Road
Palm Beach, Florida 33480
Tel.: (407) 655-1192, Fax: (407) 655-2106

Design Center of America
1855 Griffin Road, B-340
Dania, Florida 33004
Residential and commercial interior designer, architectural designer.
Fee structure: varies according to project, available upon request.
*Pages 66-67*

***Annick Presles***
La Maison Fleurie, Inc.
The Paramount, 139 North County Road, Ste. 20A
Palm Beach, Florida 33480
Tel.: (407) 833-1083, Fax: (407) 833-9318
Caracas, Venezuela office: Tel.: (582) 263-9712
Residential, office, hotel and restaurant interior design; party design.
Fee structure: varies according to project, available upon request.
*Pages 148-149*

***Carlos A. Profet***
Inarch N.V.
Vondellaan 19-B
Oranjestad, Aruba
Tel.: (297) 8-25677, Fax: (297) 8-32574
Office, contract and residential interior design.
Fee structure: varies according to project.
*Pages 206-207*

***Leticia Chaves Ray***
Mariscal Estigarribia 1636
Asuncion, Paraguay
Tel.: (595) 21-200-612, Fax: (595) 21-210-846
Residential, office and restaurant interior design.
Fee structure: varies according to project.
*Pages 150-151*

***Gloria Roberts, ISID***
Gloria Balogh Interiors
1733 Massachusetts Avenue
Riverside, California 92507
Tel.: (909) 787-9279, Fax: (909) 683-7291
Residential and office interior design.
Fee structure: available upon request.
*Pages 108-109*

***Chavivan Rujimora***
Design 103 Ltd.
7th-9th, 14/F, Asoke Towers Office Building
219 Asoke Road, Bangkok 10110, Thailand
Tel.: (66) 2-260-0160
Fax: (66) 2-259-0489, 2-259-1191
Residential, office and clubhouse interior design.
Fee structure: varies according to project, available upon request.
*Pages 208-209*

***Sandi Samole, ASID, IDG, Fl. Lic. 1B00000056***
S & B Interiors, Inc.
9700 Dixie Highway, Suite 1030
Miami, Florida 33156
Tel.: (305) 670-4148, 661-1577
Fax: (305) 661-2722
Residential, office and medical facilities interior design.
Fee structure: varies according to project, available upon request.
*Pages 68-69*

***Barbara Marie Sande***
Claremont Antique & Interior, Inc.
3529 Boyer Circle
Lafayette, California 94549
Tel.: (510) 299-1176
Residential and commercial interior design.
Fee structure: available upon request.
*Pages 110-111*

***Darryl H. Savage***
DHS Designs, Inc.
86 Maryland Avenue
Annapolis, Maryland 21401
Tel.: (410) 280-3466, Fax: (410) 647-6816
Residential, hotel and restaurant interior design.
Fee structure: hourly fee, plus percentage of net purchases.
*Pages 70-71*

***Yozo Shibata, JIA***
Kanko Kikaku Sekkeisha, Yozo Shibata & Associates
No. 17 Mori Bldg., 1-26-5 Toranomon
Minato-ku, Tokyo 105, Japan
Tel.: (81) 3-3507-0376, Fax: (81) 3-3507-0386
Hotel and restaurant interior design.
Fee structure: available upon request.
*Pages 210-211*

***Vipwal Singhakowin***
Design 103 Ltd.
7th-9th, 14/F, Asoke Towers Office Building
219 Asoke Road, Bangkok 10110, Thailand
Tel.: (66) 2-260-0160
Fax: (66) 2-259-0489, 2-259-1191
Residential, office and contract interior design.
Fee structure: varies according to project, available upon request.
*Pages 212-213*

***Mary L. Sorenson***
Cedar Hill Design Center
712 Cedar Street
Cedar Hill, Texas 75104
Tel.: (214) 291-2070, Fax: (214) 293-0378
Residential and office interior design.
Fee structure: varies according to project; hourly, flat rate, or retail.
*Pages 112-113*

***James Steinmeyer, ISID, ASID, CINOA***
James Steinmeyer Associates
1475-85 Calder Avenue
Beaumont, Texas 77701
Tel.: (409) 833-7007, Fax: (409) 833-7078
Residential interior design.
Fee structure: negotiated.
*Pages 114-115*

***Patricia S. Stotler***
Pat Stotler Interiors, Inc.
110 Coral Cay Drive, BallenIsles
Palm Beach Gardens, Florida 33418
Tel.: (407) 627-0527, Fax: (407) 626-7015
Residential interior design.
Fee structure: design fee with commission on discounted purchases as standard; some projects have hourly fee, depending on scope of project.
*Pages 72-73*

***Edward Turrentine, ASID***
Edward C. Turrentine Interior Design, Inc.
70 North Raymond Avenue
Pasadena, California 91103
Tel.: (818) 795-9964, Fax: (818) 795-0027
Residential, office, hotel and restaurant interior design.
Fee structure: initial consultation - no charge.
*Pages 116-117*

***Chiu-Hwa Wang***
Chiu-Hwa Wang Architect
21, Alley 12, Lane 118, Ren Ai Road, Sec. 3
Taipei, Taiwan, ROC
Tel.: (886) 2-701-2617, Fax: (886) 2-700-4489
Contract architectural and interior design.
Fee structure: varies according to project.
*Pages 152-153*

***Larry Warren***
Larry Warren Architect Ltd.
'Rose Bank' Derricks
St. James, Barbados, West Indies
Tel.: (809) 432-6392, Fax: (809) 432-2976
Architectural interior design.
Fee structure: percentage basis.
*Pages 154-155*

***John Wendover, B.A. (Hon.)***
Les Concepts Decoratifs Wendover, Inc.
3875 Saint-Urbain, Suite 611
Montreal, Quebec, Canada H2W 1V1
Tel.: (514) 281-2073
Fax: (514) 844-8843, (514) 769-5618
Residential and office interior design.
Fee structure: varies according to project.
*Pages 214-215*

***Vicki Wenger, ASID***
Beautiful Spaces, Inc.
2801 New Mexico Avenue, NW
Washington DC, 20007
Tel.: (202) 337-4463, Fax: (202) 298-8216
Residential, office, hotel and restaurant interior design.
Fee structure: available upon request.
*Pages 1, 74-75, back cover*

***Gaby Widajanti, HDII, IAI***
Ahara Prima Design Pt. Interior Design
Jl. Birah II No. 4, Kebayoran Baru
Jakarta 12120, Indonesia
Tel.: (62) 21-712-388, Fax: (62) 21-720-7432
Office, hotel, restaurant and health care interior design.
Fee structure: negotiable.
*Pages 216-217*

***Evan Williams***
DCI International
19 Surbiton Road
Kingston 10, Jamaica
Tel.: (809) 926-4288, Fax: (809) 929-2007
Residential, contract, hotel and restaurant interior design.
Fee structure: available upon request.
*Pages 218-219*

***John Wilman***
John Wilman Limited
Riverside Mills, Crawford Street
Nelson Lancashire, England BB9 7QT
Tel.: (44) 282-617-777, Fax: (44) 282-614-222
Fabric design; residential, office, hotel, restaurant and contract interior design.
Fee structure: available upon request.
*Pages 156-157*

***Ron Wilson***
Ron Wilson Designer
1235 Tower Road
Beverly Hills, California 90210
Tel.: (310) 276-0666, Fax: (310) 276-7291
Residential interior design.
Fee structure: design consultation fee, cost and one-third.
*Pages 118-119*

***Vicente Wolf***
Vicente Wolf Associates, Inc.
333 West 39 Street
New York, New York 10018
Tel.: (212) 465-0590, Fax: (212) 465-0639
Residential, office and contract interior design; product design.
Fee structure: commission 35% of cost.
*Pages 76-77*

***Susan A. Wolfe, ISID***
Casa Ambiente S.A. de C.V.
Monte Athos No. 139, Lomas de Chapultepec
11000 Mexico DF, Mexico
Tel.: (52) 5-202-0541, 5-520-8870
Fax: (52) 5-520-2050
Residential, hotel and restaurant interior design.
Fee structure: since we produce our furniture and fabrics, our fee is US$300.00 – a one time consultation charge to do the whole house.
*Pages 120-121*

***Flora Ye Ouyang***
Yei Projeto e Objeto
Rua Manoel Mendes Fernandes 29, Jardim Paulista
CEP-04507-030, Sao Paulo, Brazil
Tel.: (55) 11-887-7490, Fax: (55) 11-884-7873
Residential, office and showroom interior design; custom glass pieces, exclusive fabric upholstery.
Fee structure: available upon request.
*Pages 158-159*

***Jaci Yoap, IFDA***
Interiors by Jaci
Highway B
Pound, Wisconsin 54161
Tel.: (414) 897-3536, Fax: (414) 897-2825
Residential interior design; Oriental and European antiques.
Fee structure: varies according to project.
*Pages 220-221*

***Bettye Jordan Young***
B. Jordan Young Inc.
6565 Sunset Boulevard, Suite 321
Hollywood, California 90028
Tel.: (213) 871-4944, (800) 876-0886
Fax: (213) 876-1133
Residential and contract interior design.
Fee structure: percentage or time and expenses depending on client.
*Pages 122-123*

***Hugh Zimmern***
Leigh & Orange Ltd.
3/F, Chung Shun Bldg., 88 Hing Fat Street
Causeway Bay, Hong Kong
Tel.: (852) 806-1312, Fax: (852) 806-0343
Office, hotel and restaurant interior design.
Fee structure: available upon request.
*Pages 222-223*

# *Photographers Index*

***Russell Abraham***
Russell Abraham Photography
60 Federal Street, Suite 303
San Francisco, California 94107
Tel.: (415) 896-6400, Fax: (415) 896-6402
*Pages 106-107*

***Jamie Ardiles-Arce***
509 Madison Avenue
New York, New York 10022
Tel.: (212) 688-9191
*Back cover*

***Mark Atkinson***
Singapore
Tel.: (65) 472-2063
*Pages 222-223*

***Andrew Baran***
Innova Interiors, Inc.
7802 Davenport Street
Omaha, Nebraska 68114
Tel.: (402) 392-1115, Fax: (402) 392-0188
*Pages 78-79, 98-99*

***Gordon Beall***
4411 Bradley Lane
Chevy Chase, Maryland 20815
Tel.: (301) 229-0076, (301) 718-6238
*Pages 1, 74-75, back cover*

***Victor Benitez***
Av. Voracruz No. 38-5
06700 Mexico DF, Mexico
Tel.: (52) 5-286-2542
*Pages 120-121*

***Seth Benson***
4625 Taylor Street
Hollywood, Florida 33021
Tel.: (305) 987-9404
*Pages 68-69*

***Henry Biber***
Henry Biber Photography
P.O. Box 140331
Dallas, Texas 75214
Tel.: (214) 828-0902, Fax: (214) 828-4243
*Pages 112-113*

***Peter Blake***
New Jersey
Tel.: (201) 767-3150
*Page 13*

***Mark Boisclair***
Mark Boisclair Photography
2512 East Thomas Road, Suite One
Phoenix, Arizona 85016
Tel.: (602) 957-6997, Fax: (602) 957-8494
*Pages 94-95*

***José Bouthillette***
1404 Fullum, Apt. B
Montreal, Quebec, Canada H2K 3M1
Tel.: (514) 368-2830, Fax: (514) 368-2867
*Pages 214-215*

***John Canham***
Quadra Focus Photography
588 Waite Avenue
Sunnyvale, California 94086
Tel.: (408) 739-1465, Fax: (408) 739-9117
*Pages 102-103*

***James Chen***
James Chen Studios
1917 Anacapa Street
Santa Barbara, California 93101
Tel.: (805) 569-1849, Fax: (805) 563-2240
*Pages 100-101*

***Y.C. Chien***
265-7 Hu-Lin Street
Taipei, Taiwan, ROC
Tel.: (886) 2-726-3913, Fax: (886) 2-727-1606
*Pages 12, 202-203*

***Ok-Rei Cho***
Dae Young International
Sam-Dae Yang Building
543 Shin-Sa Dong, Kang-Nam Ku
Seoul, South Korea
Tel.: (82) 2-511-3211, Fax: (82) 2-542-1024
*Pages 164 165*

***Houng-Kuk Chun***
Artiplan House
794-8 Hannam-Dong Yongsan-Gu
Seoul, Korea
Tel.: (82) 2-795-1157, Fax: (82) 2-795-0773
*Pages 200-201*

***Langdon Clay***
Atlanta, Georgia
Tel.: (404) 257-2727
*Pages 76-77*

***Tom Cliff***
*Pages 22-23*

***Joe Colón***
Promociones del Caribe, Inc.
Edif. American Airlines
Calle López Landrón 1509, Suite 1107
Santurce, San Juan, Puerto Rico 00911
Tel.: (809) 724-4260, Fax: (809) 724-4219
*Pages 142-143*

***Daniel Design and Production***
12/F, Union Commercial Building
12-16 Lyndhurst Terrace
Central, Hong Kong
Tel.: (852) 854-4181, Fax: (852) 854-4069
*Pages 184-185*

***Mark Darley***
Mark Darley Photography
23 Midway Avenue
Mill Valley, California 94941
Tel.: (415) 381-5451
*Pages 6-7*

***Harold Davis***
*Pages 108-109*

***Robbie Davis***
Davisual Productions Ltd.
"Cabers", Westmoreland
St. James, Barbados
Tel.: (809) 422-2888, Fax: (809) 422-0576
*Pages 154-155*

***Mark Dolan***
Visual Perfection
5913 Turnbull Drive
Orlando, Florida 32822
Tel.: (407) 281-4463
*Pages 58-59*

***Steve Donisch***
500 Pueblo Trail
Wheeling, Illinois 60090
Tel.: (708) 253-0403
*Pages 15, 60-61*

***Rainer Eickmeyer***
Suhan Fotographie
Gewerbepark Rheinpreussen
47182 Duisburg, Germany
Tel.: (49) 2066-10798, Fax: (49) 2066-13680
*Pages 186-187*

***Phillip H. Ennis***
Phillip H. Ennis Photography
98 Smith Street
Freeport, New York 11520
Tel.: (516) 379-4273, Fax: (516) 379-1126
*Inside flyleaf, pages 3, 5, 24-25, 34-35, 224*

***Dr. Adrian Erwin***
*Pages 136-137*

***Everett & Soulé***
Post Office Box 150674
Altamonte Springs, Florida 32715-0674
Tel.: (407) 831-4183
*Pages 50-51*

***Timothy Fields***
Tim Fields photography
916 Dartmouth Glen Way
Baltimore, Maryland 21212
Tel.: (410) 323-7831
*Pages 44-45*

***Martin Fine***
Martin Fine Photography, Inc.
10072 Larwin Avenue #1
Chatsworth, California 91311
Tel.: (818) 341-7113
*Pages 116-117*

***Dan Forer***
1970 NE 149th Street
North Miami, Florida 33181
Tel.: (305) 949-3131
*Pages 28-29, 66-67*

***Keith Franklin***
S.C.L. Imaging Group Ltd.
190 Milner Avenue
Scarborough, Ontario, Canada M1S 5B6
Tel.: (416) 293-9943, Fax: (416) 293-1064
*Pages 18-19*

***Demosthenes Perry C. Gabac Jr.***
Technical Assistant to Mr. Khalid M. Khidr
Art Center
Post Office Box 14191
Jeddah, Saudi Arabia 21426
Tel.: (966) 2-683-5002, Fax: (966) 2-682-4934
*Pages 138-139*

***Edward Gohlich***
Edward Gohlich, Photographer
P.O. Box 180919
Coronado, California 92178
Tel.: (619) 423-4237, Fax: (619) 423-0493
*Pages 84-85*

***Eduardo Gonzalez***
Photographer Eduardo Gonzalez
Canada No. 905, Col. Vista Hermosa
Monterrey NL 64620, Mexico
Tel.: (52) 918-348-5623, Fax: (52) 918-348-5623
*Pages 170-171*

***Ramon Guerrero***
(in memoriam)
*Pages 16-17*

***Anne Gummerson***
Anne Gummerson Photography
811 S. Ann Street
Baltimore, Maryland 21231
Tel.: (410) 732-4429
*Pages 70-71*

***Seow Cheong Heng***
Xiao Photo Workshop
Block 104, Geylang East Avenue 3, #02-232
Republic of Singapore 1438
Tel.: (65) 743-4831, Fax: (65) 841-0284
*Pages 160-161, 204-205*

***Jonathan Hillyer***
Jonathan Hillyer Photography, Inc.
2604 Parkside Drive, NE
Atlanta, Georgia 30305
Tel.: (404) 841-6679, Fax: (404) 841-9088
*Pages 46-47*

***Val Ihde***
Val Ihde Photographers
805 Sixth Avenue
Menominee, Michigan 49858
Tel.: (906) 864-2369
*Pages 220-221*

***Michael Irving***
*Pages 110-111*

***Arthur Kan***
7 Cross Lane, First Floor
Wanchai, Hong Kong
Tel.: (852) 834-1908, Fax: (852) 828-4913
*Pages 126-127*

***Kaplan Photography***
6633 Moly Drive
Falls Church, Virginia 22046
Tel.: (703) 893-1660, Fax: (703) 533-0820
*Page 74*

***Bill LaFevor***
Bill LaFevor Architectural Photography
Nashville, Tennessee
Tel.: (615) 297-9711
*Pages 172-173*

***Warren Leon, Jr.***
Industrial and Commercial Photograher
Post Office Box 55-1017
Panama City, Panama
Tel.: (507) 63-9145
*Pages 134-135*

***James Levin***
45 West 21st Street
New York, New York 10010
Tel.: (212) 242-5337, Fax: (212) 255-5914
*Pages 10-11, 64-65*

***Nathaniel Lieberman***
*Pages 190-191*

***David Duncan Livingston***
David Duncan Livingston, Photographer
483 Greenwich Street
San Francisco, California 94133
Tel.: (415) 392-2465, Fax: (415) 398-3312
*Pages 90-91*

***Alejandro Lopez***
Fotograficos Alex
Gregorio Davila 34
S.H. Guadalajara, Jalisco, Mexico
Tel.: (52) 95-36-263024, Fax: (52) 95-36-263816
*Pages 188-189*

***Fernando Rafael Luidens***
Check Point Color N.V.
Columbusstraat #10
Oranjestad, Aruba
Tel.: (297) 8-22284, Fax: (297) 8-38424
*Pages 206-207*

***David Luttrell***
David Luttrell Photography
Knoxville, Tennessee
Tel.: (615) 688-1430
*Page 173*

***Jim Madden***
4707 Dayton Boulevard, Suite E
Chattanooga, Tennessee 37415
Tel.: (615) 875-4052
*Pages 62-63*

***Scott McDonald***
Hedrich-Blessing
11 West Illinois Street
Chicago, Illinois 60610
Tel.: (312) 321-1151, Fax: (312) 351-1165
*Pages 176-177*

***Skip Meachen***
Photography by Skip Meachen
101 Matthews Point North
Hilton Head Island, South Carolina 29928
Tel.: (803) 681-2918
*Pages 52-53*

***Carlos Miller***
Estudio Miller
Insurgentes Sur #634, Col. del Valle
Mexico DF 03100, Mexico
Tel.: (52) 5-543-8320, 5-523-3222
*Pages 96-97*

***Allen Mims***
Mims Studios
2258 Young Avenue
Memphis, Tennessee 38104
Tel.: (901) 725-4040, Fax: (901) 725-7643
*Pages 42-43*

***Derry Moore***
Derry Moore Photography
400 Ledbury Road
London, England W11 2AB
Tel.: (44) 71-229-5950, 71-221-1183
Fax: (44) 71-221-8135
*Pages 122-123*

***Juca Moraes***
Rua Francisco Otaviano 60, Apto. 112
Copacabana CEP 22080, Brazil
Tel.: (55) 2-267-9735
*Pages 144-145*

***Alberto Moreno Guzman***
Morena 213-B-101, Col. Del Valle
Mexico DF, Mexico
Tel.: (52) 5-543-2185
*Pages 168-169, 178-179*

***Dadi Motiwalla***
Motiwalla Photographics
Post Office Box 1579
Dubai, United Arab Emirates
Tel.: (971) 4-213-037, Fax: (971) 4-221-609
*Pages 124-125, 146-147*

***Rob Muir***
Rob Muir Photography
Post Office Box 42809-404
Houston, Texas 77042
Tel.: (713) 784-7420
*Pages 114-115*

***John Ngai***
1126 Park Hill Street
Berkeley, California 94708
*Pages 152-153*

***Mary E. Nichols***
Tel.: (310) 935-3080
*Pages 86-87, 118-119*

***John Parsekian***
John Parsekian Photography
5 Lawrence Street, Bldg. 15
Bloomfield, New Jersey 07003
Tel.: (201) 748-9717
*Pages 54-55*

***Picture This & That***
Lot 3.10, 1/F, Central Square
Jalan Hang Kasture
Kuala Lumpur 50050, Malaysia
Tel.: (60) 3-201-2448, Fax: (60) 3-201-2439
*Pages 174-175*

***Thakerng Pringpuangkeo***
Bangkok, Thailand
*Pages 208-209, 212-213*

***Bill Reeves***
Monochrome Photography
2500 N. Van Dorn, Suite 317
Alexandria, Virginia 22302
Tel.: (703) 379-0437
*Pages 40-41*

***Frank Ritter***
Tel.: (914) 831-3380
*Pages 56-57*

***Richard K. Robinson***
Post Office Box 53106
Washington DC 20009
Tel.: (202) 234-2103
*Pages 32-33*

***Armando Rosales***
El Saltillence
Mexico DF, Mexico
Tel.: (52) 5-547-2450
*Pages 88-89*

***Kim Sargent***
Sargent and Associates
1235 U.S. Highway One
Juno Beach, Florida 33408
Tel.: (407) 627-4711
*Pages 72-73*

***Durston Saylor***
H. Durston Saylor, Inc.
14 East 4th Street, #1118
New York, New York 10012
Tel.: (212) 228-2468, Fax: (212) 228-2846
*Front cover, pages 2, 4, 26-27, back cover*

***David Schilling***
David Schilling Photography
1816-D Briarwood Industrial Court
Atlanta, Georgia 30329
Tel.: (404) 636-1399
*Pages 48-49*

***Wolfgang Schumann***
Wolfgang Schumann Werbefotografie
Ahornallee 50
14050 Berlin, Germany
Tel.: (49) 30-302-5350, Fax: (49) 30-301-9509
*Pages 192-193*

***Tony Soluri***
Tony Soluri Photography
1147 West Ohio, #403
Chicago, Illinois 60622
Tel.: (312) 243-6580
*Pages 20-21*

***Voravut Suamonruttanakul***
Hook Press & Design Co., Ltd.
539/1 Sukhumvit 71 Road, Soi White Village
Bangkok 10110, Thailand
Tel.: (66) 2-381-2754, Fax: (66) 2-381-2755
*Pages 132-133*

***Robert Suddarth***
Robert Suddarth Photography
3402 73rd Street, Suite D
Lubbock, Texas 79424
Tel.: (806) 795-4553
*Pages 104-105*

***Rudi Sugiarto***
Jalan Cimandiri No. 24
Jakarta 10330, Indonesia
Tel.: (62) 21-310-2173, 21-322-718
*Pages 216-217*

***Ryuzo Tanabe***
Tanabe Ryuzo Photo Studio
Roppongi Royal Mansion #501, 6-8-14, Roppongi
Minato-ku, Tokyo 106, Japan
Tel.: (81) 3-3408-1664
*Pages 194-195*

***Fifi Tong***
Fifi Studio
Rua Justina 583
CEP-04545, Sao Paulo, Brazil
Tel.: (55) 11-852-1419
*Pages 158-159*

***Paolo Utimpergher***
Via Messina 1
Milan, Italy
Tel.: (39) 2-336-348-018
*Pages 140-141*

***John Vaughan***
319 Arkansas Street
San Francisco, California 94107
Tel.: (415) 550-7898, Fax: (415) 550-8024
*Pages 82-83*

***José Manuel Vidaurre***
Caracas, Venezuela
Tel.: (582) 781-1841
*Pages 148-149*

***Peter Vitale***
157 East 71st Street
New York, New York 10021
Tel.: (212) 888-6409
*Pages 30-31, 36-37*

***Jack Weinhold***
Jack Weinhold Photography
15 South Shore Road
Nantucket, Massachusetts 02554
Tel.: (508) 228-5242, Fax: (508) 228-5588
*Pages 38-39*

***Mark Wilman***
Mark Wilman Photography
Brookfield Church, Brookfield
Glossop, Derby, England SK13 9JE
Tel.: (44) 457-866-667, Fax: (44) 457-866-667
*Pages 156-157*

---

We have endeavored to assure the accuracy of the information provided in these indexes. We welcome information on any oversight, which will be corrected in subsequent printings.

---



---

*In addition to the designers and photographers who have participated in the publication of this book, special thanks is also offered to all those others who provided valuable assistance in its creation: Don Burnett, M.A., Carla Copenhaven, Ph.D., Jane Huang and Janet Showalter (editorial); Marie Germe and Meaghan Maher (research); Richard Cromwell, Corinne Zink Kopen, Chris Mingear, and Beth Robinson (production); the American Institute of Architects, the American Society of Interior Designers, the Institute of Business Designers, and the International Society of Interior Designers (text material). I would also like to thank Geoffrey Bradfield, Alfredo Brito, Samuel Botero, Michael de Santis, Rodger Dobbel, Myriel Hiner, Cynthia Leftwich, Michael Love, Rod Maxwell, Carol Meltzer, Wajih Naccache, Joshua Pan, Ed Poole and Vicki Wenger for the photographs they provided for various introductory pages, and especially Vicente Wolf for graciously taking the time to write the Foreword of this edition.*

*– J. L. P.*